Our reliance is in love of liberty which God has planted in us. Our defense is in the spirit which prized liberty as the heritage of all men, in all lands everywhere.

Abraham Lincoln
Speech at Edwardsville, Ill.
September 11, 1858

Landmarks of Liberty

HAMMOND®
INCORPORATED

Acknowledgments

The publishers of *Landmarks of Liberty* gratefully acknowledge the assistance of the National Park Service, Department of the Interior, in the creation of this work.

Picture credits — United States Department of the Interior, National Park Service: title page (Geo. Washington statue), pages 9, 10, 11, 18, 19, 20, 22, 24, 25, 27, 28, 42, 43, 50, 51, 55, 65, 67, 68, 69, 70, 72, 73, 74, 75, 79, 84, 86, 88, 90. Kentucky Department of Public Information: page 8. National Geographic Photographer George F. Mobley, courtesy U.S. Capitol Historical Society: title page (aerial view), page 16. J. Waring Stinchcomb: pages 12, 17, 30, 33, 46, 49, 53, 54, 76, 80, 83. Donald C. Bacheller: page 35. Howard Fogg painting, courtesy Union Pacific Railroad: page 39. Pennsylvania Department of Commerce: page 41. Walter H. Miller: page 48. Kenneth Engler: page 56. Paul W. Nesbit: page 59. Ernest J. Dupuy: page 60. Robert L. Glore: page 64.

Title page illustrations: George Washington statue at Federal Hall, New York City and aerial view of U.S. Capitol, Washington, D.C.

LANDMARKS OF LIBERTY is a publication of
HAMMOND INCORPORATED,
Maplewood, New Jersey
MCMLXX
LIBRARY OF CONGRESS CATALOG CARD NO. 77-114691
PRINTED IN THE UNITED STATES OF AMERICA

Contents

1. Abraham Lincoln Birthplace 8
2. Appomattox Court House 10
3. Capitol Building 12
4. Federal Hall 18
5. Fort McHenry 20
6. Fort Sumter 26
7. George Washington Birthplace 30
8. Gettysburg Battlefield 34
9. Golden Spike Historic Site 38
10. Independence Hall 40
11. Jamestown 46
12. Jefferson National Expansion Memorial 50
13. Lincoln Memorial 52
14. Mesa Verde Cliff Dwellings 56
15. Minute Man Statue 60
16. Mount Rushmore 64
17. Saratoga Battlefield 66
18. Statue of Liberty 70
19. Thomas Jefferson Memorial 76
20. Tomb of the Unknown Soldier 80
21. Washington Monument 82
22. Wright Brothers Memorial 88

Index 92

1
Abraham Lincoln Birthplace

Hodgenville, Ky.

On a raw frontier farm of rolling land on the edge of "the Barrens," in the cabin by the Sinking Spring, was born the man whose strides carried him awkwardly, yet majestically, over a path which began in common Kentucky clay and ended in immortality.

THE LINCOLN FAMILY

At the close of the Revolution, during Indian wars and raids, the Lincoln family moved to the frontier region of Kentucky. The father of Abraham Lincoln, the sixteenth President, was Thomas Lincoln; his grandfather was Abraham, for whom he was named.

About 1800, Thomas Lincoln settled in Elizabethtown and during the next few years was a hard-working and industrious man of that community, acquiring a reputation as a carpenter.

On June 10, 1806, Thomas Lincoln filed a declaration of intention to marry Nancy Hanks, and 2 days later, they were married by Rev. Jesse Head. The newly married couple made their home in Elizabethtown. Here their first child, Sarah, was born in 1807.

The image of Nancy Hanks is blurred and uncertain to us of this generation. Although her physical features left no definite impression upon the minds of those who years later tried to recall her image, there is an almost unanimous agreement among these witnesses concerning her mental and spiritual attributes. That she was possessed of a fine native intelligence, courage, and a morality above reproach and that she was kind and affectionate seem fairly clear.

THE BIRTHPLACE OF ABRAHAM LINCOLN

On December 12, 1808, Thomas Lincoln bought for $200 in cash the 300-acre Sinking Spring Farm, situated a few miles south of Hodgen's Mill. Here, he and his wife and their infant daughter took up their abode in a one-room log cabin near a large limestone spring of cool water which had given its name to the place. It was in this one-room log cabin near the Sinking Spring that the child, Abraham, was born to Thomas and Nancy Hanks Lincoln on February 12, 1809.

The Lincolns lived about 2½ years at the birthplace site, which eventually was lost to them because of a defective land title. Prior to midsummer in 1811 they moved to a farm on Knob Creek, about 10 miles to the northeast. Their residence there lasted only a few years, for in November or December 1816, Thomas Lincoln left Kentucky and made a new home in the wilderness settlement of

Marble Memorial building contains old log cabin (photo right) where according to tradition Abraham Lincoln was born.

Little Pigeon Creek, about 16 miles north of the Ohio River, in Indiana. Nancy Hanks Lincoln, the mother of Abraham, lived only about 2 years after they moved to Indiana. An epidemic came to the little settlement on Pigeon Creek and, while attending the stricken, she herself was taken ill and died within a week, on October 5, 1818. The mother of Abraham Lincoln was buried in an unmarked grave in a little clearing in the deep woods.

THE BIRTHPLACE CABIN

From 1861 to the present, the history of the log cabin which is now displayed within the memorial building is fairly clear. Its history prior to 1861 is a matter of controversy and doubt. Nor is there conclusive evidence concerning the specific location of the original cabin. Certain testimony indicates that it stood on top of the knoll where the memorial building is now situated; still other that it stood under the knoll, a short distance from the Sinking Spring and about on a level with it.

Dr. George Rodman was the first individual to become interested in preserving the cabin. In March 1861, he bought a log cabin standing on the birthplace farm and moved it a little over a mile to the north and reerected it on his own farm. Here it remained until 1895, when it was purchased by a representative of A. W. Dennett of New York and returned to the Lincoln farm where 110½ acres of land had been purchased about this time by Dennett. In the succeeding years the cabin was dismantled and the logs carefully marked and taken to various expositions throughout the country. Eventually the cabin was stored in the basement of the old Poppenhusen mansion at College Point, Long Island, N.Y. It remained there until 1906 when it was purchased by the Lincoln Farm Association. It was then sent to Louisville under a military escort where, after being reerected as a feature of the Louisville Homecoming celebration, it again went into storage. In 1909, the cabin was moved temporarily to the birthplace farm for the ceremonies attending the laying of the cornerstone of the memorial building. In 1911, upon completion of this structure, the cabin was taken on the last of its travels back to the site of its origin and reerected within the memorial building.

THE FARM AND THE MEMORIAL BUILDING

In 1904, the Lincoln Farm Association was formed for the purpose of raising funds by popular subscription to purchase the birthplace and make it a national memorial. Richard Lloyd Jones, then managing editor, and Robert J. Collier, publisher of Collier's Weekly, were its leading members.

The memorial building, designed by John Russell Pope and built of Connecticut pink granite and Tennessee marble, was constructed by the Lincoln Farm Association in the years 1909-11 through funds raised by popular subscription. Over 100,000 citizens, many of them school children, contributed to this fund. The cornerstone of the building was laid on February 12, 1909, the 100th anniversary of Lincoln's birth, and it was dedicated on November 9, 1911. On April 16, 1916, the Lincoln Farm Association deeded its holdings to the United States of America.

Abraham Lincoln Birthplace National Historic Site comprises 116½ acres of land, nearly 100 acres of which were included in the original Thomas Lincoln farm. Here are the memorial building housing the traditional Lincoln birthplace log cabin, the Sinking Spring, and the ancient boundary oak tree which was a landmark at the time of Lincoln's birth. The area was established as a National Park in 1916. The designation was changed to Abraham Lincoln Birthplace National Historic Site in 1959.

2
Appomattox Court House

Appomattox, Va.

For 9 months, from June 1864 to April 1865, Grant's Army of the Potomac besieged Richmond and Petersburg, last strongholds of Lee's army and the Confederate Government. The campaign was a study in attrition. As losses, captures, and desertion thinned Lee's defensive line, Grant was strengthened by the arrival of armies from other theaters. In the last important battle of the war, at Five Forks on April 1, a Union victory compelled Lee to evacuate his position to save his army. The next day the Confederates marched away from Petersburg and headed west, intending to pick up rations at Amelia Court House, then proceed down the railroad to Danville, and ultimately join forces with Gen. Joseph E. Johnston, operating in North Carolina. To continue effective resistance, Lee had to be resupplied and strengthened.

Warfare now became a matter of rapid movement, as Lee retreated and Grant pursued aggressively. For the Confederates, disaster piled upon disaster. At Amelia Court House, Lee's hungry and exhausted veterans found no rations waiting. At Jetersville a strong Union force blocked the retreat south and caused Lee to turn west toward Lynchburg. At Sayler's Creek the Confederate rearguard was cut off and over 6,000 men captured. At Farmville, Lee barely beat Grant across the Appomattox, but the race was so close that the main bridge went undestroyed, and Grant continued to press hard on Lee's heels.

By Saturday night, April 8, in camp just east of Appomattox Court House, Lee realized that his army was trapped. The men were without shoes and clothing, the animals without forage. For a while Lee thought there might be a slim chance to cut through the rapidly moving Federals and resume the march to Lynchburg. But the light of Union campfires to the south, east, and west dimmed that hope.

Opposite
McLean House where Lee met Grant to discuss terms of surrender.

Right
The surrender room on the first floor of the McLean House.

At a council of war that evening, Lee and his generals decided on one last try the next morning. If only cavalry lay ahead of them, then perhaps they could break out. At dawn the next day, Lee sent Gen. Fitzhugh Lee with cavalry and Gen. John B. Gordon with infantry to drive back Union horsemen seen on the ridge west of the village of Appomattox Court House. They brushed aside the cavalry, only to run into Union Gen. E.O.C. Ord's infantry. Ord stopped the Confederates cold, pushed them back, and by 10 a.m. had themselves advanced to the western outskirts of Appomattox Court House.

Lee now faced his last decision on a field of battle. As an informal truce brought quiet along the battleline, Lee sought to arrange a meeting with Grant to discuss surrender terms. His only alternative was more futile bloodshed and the destruction of his fast dwindling force.

About 12:15 p.m. Lt. Col. Orville E. Babcock, aide to Grant, delivered a note to Lee informing him of Grant's willingness to confer on terms. At Lee's direction, Col. Charles Marshall, his aide, went off to find a suitable meeting place. A messenger finally found Grant and turned him toward Appomattox Court House, where Lee, Marshall, and Babcock now waited in the parlor of Wilmer McLean's house.

Grant arrived on the village outskirts about 1:30 and was directed to a red-brick house in a locust grove. Walking his horse to the house, he dismounted and climbed the wide steps. For a conquering general on so momentous an occasion, Grant was casually dressed. He wore the uniform of a private soldier, with the tacked-on insignia straps of a lieutenant general, and his pants and boots were spattered with mud.

Rising when Grant entered, Lee started across the room and the two shook hands briefly with quiet greetings. Lee, by contrast, was dressed faultlessly, with a sash of deep red silk and his finest sword buckled to his side. Then Grant's staff entered the room and lined the walls. After some talk, mainly of old army days, Lee turned the conversation to the matter at hand. Grant's terms were generous: all men would be set free upon their promise never to take up arms against the U.S. Government again; officers could keep their sidearms and horses; and men in the ranks who claimed to own horses or mules could keep them, as Grant put it, "to work their little farms."

"This will have the best possible effect upon the men," said Lee. "It will be very gratifying and will do much toward conciliating our people."

The terms and acceptance were drafted in final form and signed by Lee and Grant. By 4 o'clock the ceremony was over.

Lee stepped out on the porch oblivious of the Union officers standing respectfully with bared heads in the yard. "Traveller," his horse, was brought up, and Lee, roused from his reverie, mounted, raised his hat, and slowly rode through the village and back across the river. There he told his men that they had been surrendered. The date was Palm Sunday, April 9, 1865.

Three days later Lee's veterans marched as a unit for the last time. Crossing the river at a shallow ford, they filed up the steep hill and past lines of blue-clad soldiers to stack their arms at the eastern edge of the village. Many wept as they laid their battle flags across the weapons, but some tore the banners into bits, rather than surrender them, and passed out the pieces. All told, 28,231 Confederates were paroled at Appomattox, as 80,000 Federals watched silently or stood guard in the village.

The war was over, an era had spent itself ... thoughts now turned to the problems of peace and reunion.

3
Capitol Building

Washington, D. C.

When this Nation emerged victorious from its struggle for independence, it had no site for its Federal Government. On April 30, 1783, six years before the Constitution was ratified, the first action was begun to find a permanent seat of government. Various sites were offered, and many plans were discussed.

On July 16, 1790, after Maryland and Virginia donated generous portions of land along the Potomac River, Congress by law established the Federal District, now known as the District of Columbia, as the permanent seat of our Government.

The first public communication on record concerning arrangements for laying out the new capital city was penned by General Washington himself on March 11, 1791. In a subsequent letter of April 30, 1791, he referred to it as the Federal City. The name Washington was adopted about four months later, probably without the General's knowledge.

The new District encompassed an area of 10 miles square. Its first cornerstone was placed at Jones Point near Alexandria, Virginia, on April 15, 1791, by Commissioners Carroll and Stuart. Major Pierre Charles L'Enfant was selected by President Washington to prepare plans for the city.

His design, at once publicly acclaimed unique and artistic, called for broad avenues, ample parks, with circles and squares reserved for monuments to national heroes. The Executive Mansion and the Capitol were the first two sites chosen by Washington and L'Enfant, the latter site atop Jenkins Hill one mile southeast of the former. These two points were to serve as hubs of giant wheels, from which avenues would emanate like huge spokes.

In Jenkins Hill, the young Frenchman saw a "pedestal waiting for a monument." No one can deny that it has more than adequately served that purpose, for the Capitol of the United States, majestic as it is atop this hill, is a fitting monument to the oldest republic in the world today. Viewed either under the blue skies by day or brilliantly illuminated against the dark of night, the great dome of this building, topped by the Statue of Freedom with the flag of the United States unfurled before it, is an impressive spectacle.

Of the many plans submitted for the Capitol, that of Dr. William Thornton, an amateur architect, drew the highest praise from President Washington and Secretary of State Jefferson. He was awarded a $500 prize.

BUILDING THE CAPITOL

Construction began early in 1793, and on September 18 of that year President Washington laid the cornerstone. The Capitol was built in five sections, but the central part of the building was not the first completed. The first section was the wing joining the rotunda area on the north, started in 1793 and occupied in 1800. The central unit was begun in 1818, with the rotunda area constructed by 1827 and the entire unit finished in 1829; the House wing was begun in 1851 and ready for occupancy in 1857; the Senate wing was also started in 1851, but was not ready for occupancy until 1859.

When the first section was completed in 1800, lawmakers of the young Republic moved their quarters from Philadelphia to Washington. Thirty-two Senators and one hundred six Representatives crowded into the north wing with all the records, furniture, and archives that the new Nation possessed. The Supreme Court, composed of six Justices, met in the north wing in February 1801.

Disaster struck the Capitol on August 24, 1814. It was burned by the British at the height of the second war between the United States and England. United States troops, suffering defeat at the outskirts of the Capital City, were considerably demoralized. American forces had been ordered to retreat to the Capitol and defend it, and then a second order directed a retreat to Georgetown. As the Capitol was left unguarded, Admiral Cockburn easily entered it with a small detachment of British troops.

Thousands of priceless documents, books, and works of art were destroyed in the fire. The Capitol itself would have been demolished but for a small group of determined patriots and a heavy rainstorm that helped to quench the flames.

Some individuals, previously dissatisfied with the location of the Federal City, used this incident in an attempt to change the seat of government. President James Madison was hard pressed to retain the Capital City on the banks of the Potomac, and after much heated debate Congress defeated the project for removal and work was begun to rebuild the Capitol.

During this period when its legislative halls were being restored, Congress met first at Blodgett's Hotel on E Street between Seventh and Eighth Streets Northwest, moved at a later date to a hastily constructed building known as the *Brick Capitol* which stood on the site of the present United States Supreme Court Building. This temporary *Capitol* was erected by a group of private citizens as an inducement to keep the Federal Government in Washington. It was December of 1819 before Congress could meet again in the Capitol and carry on the Nation's business from within its walls.

Having completed the restoration of the north and south wings, Capitol Architect Charles Bulfinch began construction on the center section. Completed in 1829, it was capped with a low wooden dome covered with copper. Since neither the House nor Senate exercised jurisdiction over the rotunda area at the time, hucksters under the guise of "exhibitions" soon turned the place into a glorified market place for selling everything from ribbons to pianos.

By 1850 it was evident that the two Houses of Congress had outgrown their existing quarters. The decision was made to construct entirely new chambers on both sides of the Capitol. Work had not progressed far on the Senate and House additions when it became obvious that these marble extensions were going to dwarf the central dome. Thus, in 1855 the brick and wooden structure was removed to make way for the tremendous cast and wrought iron dome we know today.

The dome's weight is estimated to be almost nine million pounds. The outer metal shell makes it extremely susceptible to the sun, and it sways as a result of temperature variations. In 1865 vibratory experiments were conducted which found the dome to oscillate as much as three to four inches.

Watching the dome take shape over the rotunda during the Civil War, President Lincoln was said to have made this comment: "If people see the Capitol going on it will be a sign to them that we intend the Union shall go on."

On December 2, 1863, the Statue of Freedom took her watch over the Nation's Capital City. The placement of this symbol of liberty atop the Capitol dome and the unfurling of the Flag of the United States were heralded by a 35-gun salute from Capitol Hill, while answering salutes echoed from the 12 fortifications surrounding the city.

The House occupied its new chamber in 1857, the Senate in 1859. The old House Chamber was designated Statuary Hall in 1864. Into the vacated Senate Chamber from the floor below moved the Justices of the Supreme Court. There they were to remain until 1935 when the present magnificent Supreme Court Building was completed across from the Capitol Grounds.

RECENT CHANGES

Under the authority of a law enacted in 1956, Congress provided for the extension, reconstruction, and replacement of the east-central portion of the Capitol Building. Under the approved plans, a new front in marble, faithfully reproducing the design of the old sandstone front, has been constructed 32.6 feet east of the old front. The east walls of the connections between the central front and the Senate and House Wings were also reproduced and extended 44.11 feet. The old sandstone walls have remained in place and become a part of the interior wall construction.

WORKS OF ART IN THE CAPITOL

America's Capitol Building is more than a place for the conduct of governmental business: it is a gallery of beautiful works of art. Not the least of these are the walls and ceilings of many of the buildings corridors and rooms.

One man was almost solely responsible for the outstanding beauty of the Capitol's interior —Constantino Brumidi (1805-80). This Italian artist came to America from Rome in 1852 and was so appreciative of this country's role in the history of liberty that he asked permission to express his sympathetic gratitude by painting the interior of this symbol of freedom.

For more than a quarter of a century the artistry of a master was transformed into mute testimonials of his admiration for the Nation he loved above all others. Certainly the interior of the Capitol is far richer as a result of Brumidi's 22 years of labor and as a result of his devotion to his adopted

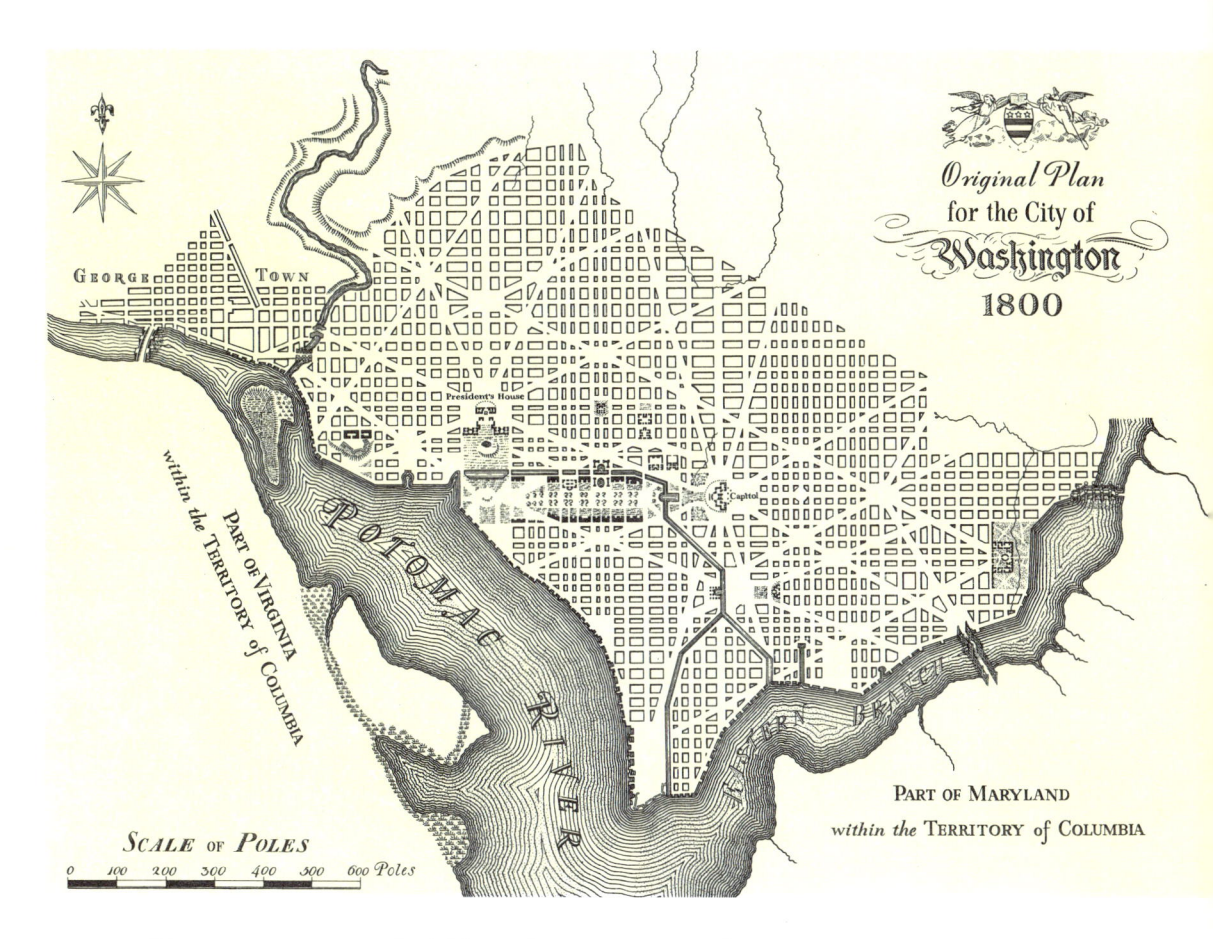

The Capitol and Executive Mansion sites were personally chosen by Washington and L'Enfant at key points in the new federal capital.

Original Plan for the City of Washington 1800

country. The most monumental of his works is the fresco on the curved canopy of the dome of the Capitol rotunda. Brumidi planned the historic figures of this painting to appear life size when viewed from the floor of the rotunda.

Below the frieze in the rotunda, also in part the work of Brumidi, are eight gigantic paintings depicting historical events in America. *The Declaration of Independence* and three others were painted by John Trumbull.

It is not possible to describe in this document the many portraits, paintings, busts, and statues displayed in the Capitol. The collection has grown, and continues to grow, in number, value, and reputation.

PRESIDENT'S ROOM

The President's Room in the Capitol Building is located in the Senate wing. It was primarily used on the 4th day of March every fourth year by Presidents to sign bills that had passed Congress during the last hours of the previous session. Their signatures were not only necessary for the act to become a law, but had to be subscribed during their term of office, which ended on that day, March 4th, at noon.

Since the ratification of the 20th Amendment, the room is no longer necessary for the purposes for which it was intended and is now used for conferences between newsmen and Senators.

Rotunda visitors gaze at works of art
in the circular hall
beneath the capitol dome.

VICE PRESIDENT'S ROOM

The Vice President's ceremonial office in the Capitol is situated at the east end of the Senators' Lobby. This room contains a wealth of precious memorabilia, in particular the famous portrait of George Washington by Rembrandt Peale, considered the best painting of Washington owned by the Government.

PRAYER ROOM

A unique addition to our Nation's Capitol is the Prayer Room. In 1954, both the Senate and the House of Representatives approved a concurrent resolution calling for the establishment of "a room with facilities for prayer and meditation for the use of Members of the Senate and House of Representatives."

TOMB AND CATAFALQUE

Beneath the rotunda of the Capitol is a crypt, and directly under this is a tomb, intended to hold the remains of the Nation's first President—but it is empty.

George Washington died in 1799, and in keeping with the desires of his will he was buried on the grounds of his beloved home at Mount Vernon. Later Congress petitioned the descendants of the Washingtons to permit removal of the bodies of both George and Martha to the Capitol.

George Washington Parke Custis, grandson of Martha Washington, granted his permission, but John A. Washington, grandnephew of the President, refused his consent, and thus the tomb remains empty to this day.

But in the tomb itself is a catafalque—a simple funeral bier draped in black broadcloth and enclosed in a glass case to protect it from accidents and dust. Abraham Lincoln was the first American President to lie in state on the catafalque in the rotunda of the Capitol. It also has served as a funeral couch for many distinguished persons and presidents.

INAUGURALS

January 20 of every fourth year is a milestone in our national history. It's the day of inauguration. A new President is to be installed. A new administration is to be established. New faces are to be introduced. The city in a gala mood extends a gracious welcome, and the inaugural visitors respond to

16

the occasion with a solemn dignity tempered with the pageantry of parade, entertainment and fun.

The East Portico of the Capitol is the traditional scene of the inaugural ceremonies. A simple but attractive platform is erected at the foot of the portico steps. It has a protective canopy and suitable seating for the Presidential party and distinguished guests. It is here that the President-elect is sworn in by the Chief Justice of the United States.

James Monroe was the first President to take the oath of office out of doors, the oath being administered in front of the Old Brick Capitol which occupied the site of the present Supreme Court Building. It was not until Andrew Jackson's inauguration, however, that the East Portico was used. Since that time most, but not all, administrations of the oath to the President-elect have been held at this historic place. A number of times inclement weather forced the ceremony into one or the other of the Congressional chambers. Franklin D. Roosevelt's fourth inaugural was held at the White House. His successor, President Truman, took the oath privately, as did some of his predecessors. The oath of the Vice President was administered in the Senate chamber prior to the enactment of the 20th Amendment. Since 1936 this proceeding has been included with the inaugural ceremonies held on the East Portico.

FLAGS

The flag of the United States flies over the Chambers of the Senate and the House when they are in session. They are raised and lowered when the two bodies begin and end daily sessions, except when either body, at the close of the day's activities, for parliamentary reasons decides to recess instead of adjourning. A recess may extend over a period of calendar days by recessing from day to day. This period is referred to by the rules of each House as a legislative day. Then the flag will fly continuously day and night until the House in recess decides to adjourn. Under authority of a law enacted in 1894, provision was made for flags to be flown over the east and west fronts of the Capitol.

During World War I requests came to Congress from all parts of the country urging that the United States flag be flown continuously each day over the public buildings in the city. Since that time the Stars and Stripes wave over the east and west fronts of the Capitol around the clock every day in the year. The flags, 8 by 12 feet in size, are removed only when they become worn and unfit for further use. Upon the death of a Member of Congress, all flags on the Capitol and those on the Senate and House Office Buildings are lowered to half-mast.

4 Federal Hall

New York, N.Y.

In the old New York City Hall on this site occurred some of the most momentous events in American history: the trial and acquittal of John Peter Zenger, marking the first important victory in the continuing struggle for freedom of the press and freedom of speech in America; the Stamp Act Congress, angrily protesting British "taxation without representation"; the sessions of the Second Continental Congress, adopting resolutions calling the Federal Constitutional Convention at Philadelphia, adopting the Northwest Ordinance and transmitting the completed Federal Constitution to the colonial legislatures for ratification. In this building, altered and renamed Federal Hall, convened the First Congress under the Constitution, and on its balcony General Washington was inaugurated first President of the United States of America. Here the Departments of State, War, and Treasury were created; the Supreme Court came into existence; and the Congress adopted the Bill of Rights.

THE CITY HALL

The City Hall, which was destined to become the scene of so many historic events, was built in 1699-1700. Prior to that time, the city government had been quartered in the old Dutch Stadt Huys on Pearl Street, and it was late in 1703 before the functions of government were transferred to the new building.

The first important historical episodes to take place in City Hall began in 1734, when John Peter Zenger was imprisoned in its garret on a charge of publishing "seditious libels" in his newspaper, the New York *Weekly Journal*. Defended by Andrew Hamilton, one of the most brilliant lawyers in the colonies, Zenger was acquitted on August 4, 1735. This was the first significant step toward es-

Washington's inauguration at the original Federal Hall, 1789.

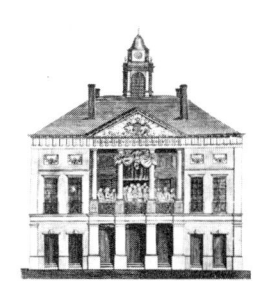

tablishing a free press and freedom of speech in America.

On October 7, 1765, the Stamp Act Congress convened at City Hall to offer the first organized opposition to England's colonial policy. Delegates from 9 of the 13 colonies participated. Before adjourning on October 26, an Address was sent to the King, petitions were directed to Parliament, and a Declaration of Rights and Grievances drawn up.

In September 1774, the First Continental Congress convening at Philadelphia in Carpenters Hall, now a part of Independence National Historical Park Project, undertook peaceful measures seeking redress of the colonies' rights and liberties violated by the British. These efforts failed. Before the Second Continental Congress convened on May 10, 1775, the American Revolution was in progress. The next year that Congress adopted the Declaration of Independence.

After the War, the Continental Congress selected New York as the seat of government and on January 11, 1785, began meeting in City Hall. Here, on February 21, 1787, the resolution calling for the Federal Constitutional Convention at Philadelphia was adopted. The Constitution, the result of 4 months' labor, was transmitted on September 28 from the City Hall to the States for ratification.

While the Constitutional Convention labored behind closed doors at Philadelphia, the Continental Congress, in New York, adopted the famous Northwest Ordinance of 1787 which provided for the government of the territory northwest of the Ohio River. In September 1788, that body designated New York City to be the capital of the United States under the Constitution. The New York City Council promptly offered the use of the City Hall and approved the expenditure of funds for putting the building in "proper order and repair."

CITY HALL BECOMES FEDERAL HALL

Under the supervision of Major Pierre Charles L'Enfant, City Hall was largely reconstructed in 1788-89. At the time the First Congress under the Constitution held its initial session, the building, then known as Federal Hall, was said to be the most beautiful in America. In an upper chamber of this building, the electoral votes were counted, on April 6, 1789, and an announcement was made of the unanimous election of George Washington as first President. On April 30, while standing on the balcony, Washington took the oath of office.

Within the next few months, the Departments of State, War, and Treasury were established by the Congress, meeting at Federal Hall. The Supreme Court was created on September 24. The Bill of Rights was adopted the following day and transmitted to the States for ratification.

In July 1790, a 10-mile-square site on the banks of the Potomac (the District of Columbia) was chosen as the site of the permanent capital. On the last day of August, the Federal Government was transferred from New York to Philadelphia, where it remained for 10 years before moving to Washington. Utilized alternately for State and city offices during the two decades following, the now crumbling Federal Hall was sold for salvage in 1812 for $425.

THE HISTORIC SITE

In 1842, the present structure, one of the most outstanding examples of Greek Revival architecture in the United States, was completed on the site of old Federal Hall. It served as the New York City Custom House until 1862 when it became the United States Sub-Treasury. Later it housed the Federal Reserve Bank of New York and a number of minor government offices. On May 26, 1939, it was designated a national historic site by the Secretary of the Interior.

5 Fort McHenry

Baltimore, Md.

Fort McHenry occupies a preeminent position among the historic shrines and monuments of our country by reason of its special meaning in American history. It was a glimpse of the American flag waving defiantly over the ramparts of Fort McHenry that inspired Francis Scott Key to compose our national anthem.

Here, where the flag flies day and night, the Stars and Stripes attains a special significance for Americans. Here on these historic ramparts one can sense and appreciate that surge of inspiration, born amid the welter of bursting bombs and blazing rockets, which compelled Francis Scott Key to create a classic expression of American ideals and patriotism. Here is symbolized the triumph of American arms and valor over a foreign invader.

FORT MCHENRY, 1794-1812

Located on the tip of a narrow peninsula, formerly called Whetstone Point, Fort McHenry separates the North West and Ferry Branches of the Patapsco River. Since all the port facilities for Baltimore were on the North West Branch, which was regarded as the city's harbor, the strategic value of Whetstone Point could not be overlooked in any plan to erect defenses to guard the water approaches to the city.

The earliest fortifications on the Point were constructed during the Revolutionary War. On March 16, 1776, local patriots reported to the Council that the fort at Whetstone was ready.

Shortly before the turn of the century, James McHenry, Secretary of War and a resident of Baltimore, was honored by the bestowal of his name on the fort. During his army career he served first as a surgeon and later as a secretary to George Washington. After the war, McHenry became active in Maryland politics and represented the State at the Constitutional Convention in Philadelphia. From its completion to the outbreak of the War of 1812, the history of the fort is routine and uneventful. Although the fort never came under enemy fire, it deterred the British cruisers which operated in Chesapeake Bay from molesting Baltimore. In 1781, Fort Whetstone, as the defense works were then called, consisted of a battery, magazine, military hospital, and barracks. After the Revolution relations with England were strained and both nations were frequently on the verge of armed conflict. Alarmed for the safety of the chief commercial city of Maryland, the House of Delegates, in 1793, passed a resolution authorizing the Governor of the State to grant permission to the Federal Government to erect a fort on Whetstone Point. Congress, in March of the following year, enacted legislation to fortify the small redoubt to defend Baltimore. John Jacob Ulrich Rivardi, an experienced artilleryman and military engineer, was directed to draw up plans for a permanent harbor defense. Governor Lee was cooperative, the local citizenry were zealous to assist, and, of utmost importance, the quality of the soil on Whetstone Point was ideal for erecting batteries.

In 1798, Maj. Louis Tousard was ordered to survey the existing defense works and submit recommendations for their improvement. He turned his plans over to a committee of local citizens who agreed to raise an additional $10,963.44 by popular subscription and to supervise the program. It is probable that the present star fort, located to the rear of the Revolutionary works, was erected during this period.

THE WAR OF 1812

In 1793, England entered the war against France, and for the next 22 years both countries were locked in a desperate life-and-death struggle into which this country was drawn. The United States attempted to define and secure recognition of its neutral rights by diplomacy. To avoid friction, embargoes and nonintercourse acts were enacted, but with indifferent success. The lack of military strength and the split in public opinion regarding the propriety of declaring war against England precluded armed hostilities. Anti-British sentiment prevailed, however, and in response to a message from President Madison a declaration of war against England was passed by Congress in June 1812.

It would be difficult to exaggerate the military unpreparedness of the United States at this time. The country was gravely deficient in arms and equipment. The army was small, disorganized, badly trained, and lacking leadership. The Navy, consisting of a handful of ships, was asked to contend with a rival which was the undisputed master of the seven seas. New England, bitterly opposed to the war, refused to furnish its share of manpower and financial support, and Congress committed a most serious blunder by failing to pass legislation for the vigorous prosecution of the war.

England was compelled to rely principally upon its navy to vanquish the United States. Late in 1812, His Majesty's Government proclaimed a blockade of the Chesapeake and Delaware Bays, and by 1813 the former had been practically converted into a British lake. Under the energetic and ruthless leadership of Rear Admiral George Cockburn, naval detachments raided many of the towns on the bay and harried their residents. The only opposition to the British was offered by Commodore Joshua Barney's small flotilla of barges and gunboats. In the summer of 1814, the

Gun drill in War of 1812 uniforms.

enemy fleet in the bay was augmented and placed under the command of Vice Admiral Alexander Cochrane. Cockburn took this opportunity to advise the army commander, Maj. Gen. Robert Ross, of the defenseless state of the city of Washington, and he urged him to take advantage of the situation. On August 19, Ross disembarked his forces at Benedict, on the Patuxent River, and on the next day moved his troops slowly toward Washington. In the meantime, a naval party under Cockburn ascended the river and compelled the Americans to burn the remnants of Barney's flotilla. At Upper Marlboro, Ross was joined by Cockburn's naval detachment, and on August 24 the combined force resumed its slow march toward the Capital. At Bladensburg the raw American militia were brushed aside and that evening the enemy entered Washington. Federal buildings were destroyed and Ross moved his troops back to the transports.

Ross and Cochrane remained for several days off the Patuxent awaiting the return of warships which had been detached on special missions. When all the scattered units had returned, Cochrane ordered the vessels to set sail, and the fleet moved northward up the bay. On September 11, the British dropped anchor at the mouth of the Patapsco just 13 miles below Baltimore, which was their next objective.

BALTIMORE, THE BRITISH OBJECTIVE

From the British point of view, Baltimore, which was larger, wealthier, and more important commercially than Washington, presented a more desirable objective than the Capital. If successful they could sequester the contents of the loaded warehouses, seize the three American warships nearing completion, and destroy the shipyards which were outfitting privateers.

Unlike Washington, Baltimore was not defenseless. Under the leadership of Maj. Gen. Samuel Smith, merchant, politician, and veteran of the Revolutionary War, it had been preparing for the expected British attack. He contrived to secure arms, ammunition, and equipment. The expenses incurred by these defense preparations were defrayed by a local committee which had raised $500,000 by popular subscription and loan. In 1813, this committee had advanced more than $40,000 to the Federal Government for the repair of Fort McHenry.

General Smith, with the consent of the French consul, removed the guns from a French warship in the harbor and had them emplaced at the fort. Two small works were erected on the Ferry Branch to protect the rear of Fort McHenry, and a small battery was set up at Lazaretto to help protect the entrance to the North West Branch.

Late in August 1814, when a British attack appeared inevitable, a special Committee of Vigilance and Safety was created. Of utmost importance, it mobilized all citizens not subject to military service for work on defenses. Under its direction a long line of strong entrenchments was erected to guard the eastern approaches to the city. To defend Baltimore, Smith had at his disposal a force of 12,000, consisting chiefly of militia, some regular army units, and about 400 sailors under Commodore John Rodgers. He decided to wage a strong defensive action. On September 11, an alarm sounded, warning the citizens of Baltimore that the British fleet had reached the Patapsco. Smith immediately ordered Brig. Gen. John Stricker to lead his brigade toward North Point to intercept the British. His final defense measure was to direct Rodgers to sink vessels across the entrances to both branches of the river.

The British strategy for the capture of Baltimore envisaged a joint land and naval attack on the city. On the morning of September 12, 1814, the troops disembarked and began to move rapidly along the road toward Baltimore. In a skirmish General Ross was mortally wounded. The command devolved upon Col. Arthur Brooke. Resuming their advance, the British army soon encountered the main body of Stricker's brigade drawn up along a line which Stricker had skillfully selected. A flanking movement forced the Americans to retire and in compliance with arrangements previously made with Smith, Stricker posted his brigade on the left, half a mile in advance of the main defense lines of Baltimore. Brooke spent the night on the battlefield of North Point, and on the following morning advanced his troops within 2 miles of the city, where they halted to await the naval cooperation deemed necessary for the successful occupation of Baltimore.

THE BOMBARDMENT OF FORT MCHENRY

To render effective assistance to Brooke's army, it was necessary for Cochrane to reduce Fort McHenry, which barred the entrance to

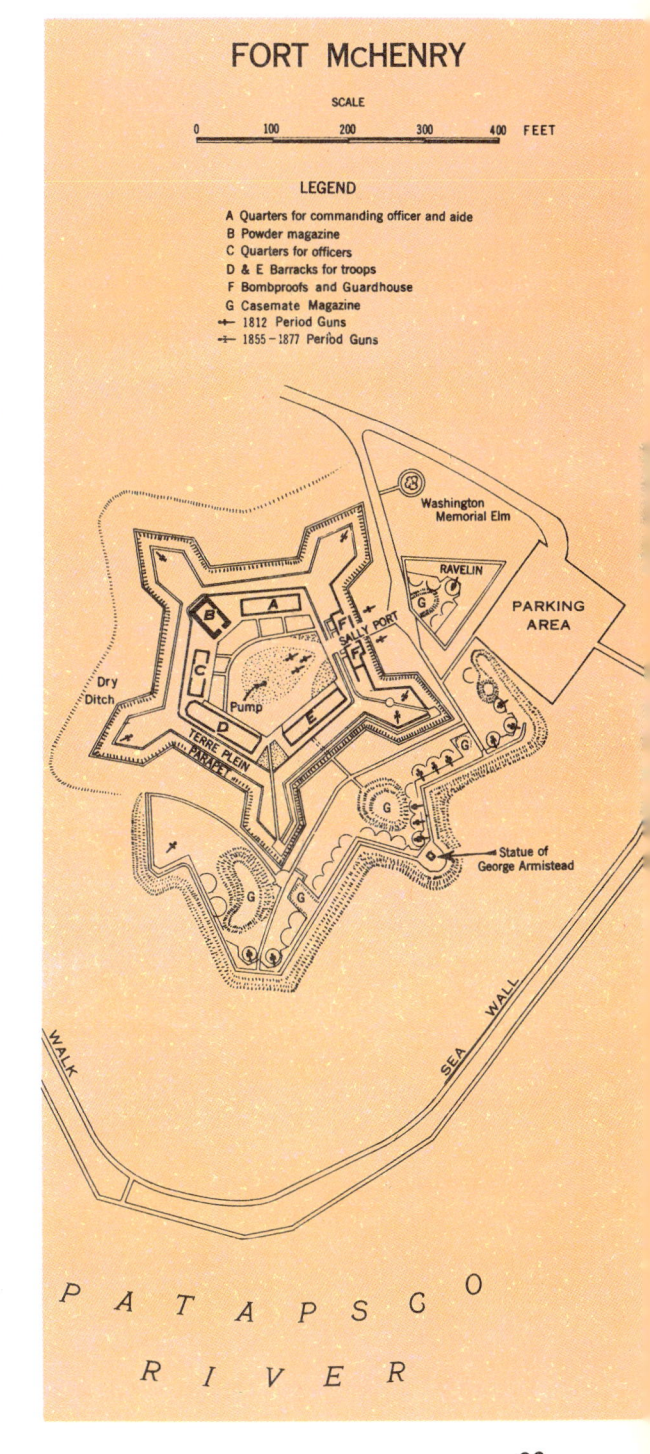

The 15-starred flag that flew over Fort McHenry was originally 42 x 30 feet. The remnant shown here is displayed in Washington.

Baltimore harbor. At dawn on September 13, 16 warships, including five bomb ships and one sloop equipped with rocket launchers, dropped anchor about 2 miles below the fort and commenced an intensive bombardment. The Americans responded with a brisk fire, but, much to their disappointment, their shot and shell fell short. In the early afternoon, a bomb landed on the southwest bastion of the fort, dismounting a gun and inflicting casualties on the crew. During the excitement, three bomb ships approached the fort but were quickly driven off by the Americans.

The critical period of the attack developed shortly after midnight when a picked British force under Captain Napier penetrated the branch of the river to the right (west) of the fort. Their mission was to storm the fort. Before they could land, however, they were detected and subjected to a withering fire from the guns of Fort McHenry and the two smaller works, Forts Babcock and Covington. The British fought back strongly with cannon and rockets. In the inky darkness, the Americans trained their weapons by the muzzle blasts of the enemy guns and the blaze of their rockets. Gradually, American fire power prevailed, and Napier was compelled to retire to the warships. The British repulse impelled Admiral Cochrane to suspend the attack. A messenger was dispatched to Colonel Brooke to inform him of the admiral's decision and to advise him to move his troops back to the transports. Brooke hastily accepted Cochrane's advice.

After a final bombardment, which lasted until 7 o'clock on the morning of the 14th, the fleet got under way and moved down river. Thus the fort, by denying the British access to the North West Branch, had frustrated the British strategy for the capture of Baltimore. The failure to take Baltimore also strengthened the position of the American peace negotiators at Ghent. Major George Armistead, commander of the fort, estimated that the British had hurled between 1,500 and 1,800 shells at the fort, of which number about 400 landed within the defense works. Two of the buildings were severely damaged, the others received slight injury. The casualty list was amazingly small. Of the 1,000 defenders, only 4 were killed and 24 injured.

THE STAR-SPANGLED BANNER

"The Star-Spangled Banner" was written in a time of great national crisis. The Capital of the United States had fallen to the enemy. Its most important Federal buildings were charred ruins in the wake of the British occupation. There seemed to be nothing separating Britain's vaunted military power from complete victory, except the small bodies of scattered and disorganized militia. American morale was at a low ebb. It required a bold

Replica of original "Star-Spangled Banner" is raised over the historic fort.

man at that time to prophesy the spiritual rebirth of the American Nation as Francis Scott Key did in "The Star-Spangled Banner."

Key, a lawyer then living in Georgetown (now a part of Washington), left for Baltimore carrying letters of introduction officially sanctioning the undertaking of freeing a friend, Dr. Beanes, from British arrest. In Baltimore, Key was joined by Col. John Skinner, who was a United States Government agent for arranging the transfer of prisoners. On September 5, 1814, the two Americans set sail from Baltimore for the Chesapeake Bay, where they expected to find the English fleet. Two days later they encountered the British on their way to attack Baltimore.

Key and Skinner boarded the *Tonnant,* flagship of the English fleet, where they were courteously received by Admiral Cochrane and General Ross. After a brief discussion Admiral Cochrane agreed to release Dr. Beanes.

However, Key and Skinner, who had become aware of the British plans for the attack on Baltimore, were informed that for security reasons they would not be allowed to return to Baltimore until the British objective had been attained. Since the H.M.S. *Tonnant* was already overcrowded with British military personnel, the two Americans were transferred to the H.M.S. *Surprize,* a light frigate, where they remained until the fleet reached the mouth of the Patapsco.

The shallow Patapsco compelled Admiral Cochrane, who wished to take personal charge of the vessels assigned to attack the fort, to transfer his flag from the large 80-gun *Tonnant* to the smaller *Surprize.* Key and Skinner were then moved back to the small American boat on which they had sailed from Baltimore, and it was from this vessel, anchored somewhere to the rear of the British fleet, that Key witnessed the attack on Fort McHenry throughout the day of September 13 and that night.

Francis Scott Key started to write the first words of "The Star-Spangled Banner" as the British terminated their attack against Fort McHenry. During his return to Baltimore, September 14, Key added lines to his poem, and that night revised and completed the original draft at the Fountain Inn, in Baltimore, where he is said to have spent the night.

Key's poem was distributed in handbill form to the citizens of Baltimore on September 15 under the title, "Defence of Fort McHenry." The first dated publication of the poem, again under the same title, appeared September 20 in the *Baltimore Patriot.* Shortly after, the title was changed to "The Star-Spangled Banner." The melody adapted for Key's poem was an old English tune entitled "To Anacreon in Heaven." On March 3, 1931, by an act of Congress, "The Star-Spangled Banner" became our official national anthem.

6
Fort Sumter

Charleston, S.C.

At 4:30 a.m., April 12, 1861, a mortar battery at Fort Johnson fired a shell that burst directly over Fort Sumter. This was the signal for a general bombardment by the Confederate batteries about Charleston Harbor. For 34 hours, April 12 and 13, Fort Sumter was battered with shot and shell. Then the Federal commander, Maj. Robert Anderson, agreed to evacuate; and, on April 14, he and his small garrison departed with the full honors of war. On the following day, President Abraham Lincoln issued a call for 75,000 militia. The tragedy of the American Civil War had begun. Both the "first shot" of April 1861 and the long siege of 1863-65 as a Confederate stronghold are commemorated today by Fort Sumter National Monument.

The War of 1812 had shown the gross inadequacy of the coastal defenses of the United States. The crowning indignity had been the burning of Washington. Accordingly, Congress set up a military Board of Engineers for Seacoast Fortifications to devise a new system of national defense. The South Atlantic coast, "especially regarded as less important," was not surveyed until 1821. Plans for a new fort in Charleston harbor opposite Fort Moultrie were drawn up and adopted in 1828. It was to be named Fort Sumter, in honor of Thomas Sumter, of South Carolina, the "Gamecock" of the Revolution. Work began that year and continued until 1834.

In 1860, thirty-two years later, Fort Sumter was still unfinished. It was a five-sided brick masonry fort designed for three tiers of guns. Its 5-foot-thick outer walls, towering nearly 50 feet above low water, enclosed a parade ground of roughly 1 acre. Along four of the walls extended two tiers of arched gunrooms. Officers' quarters lined the fifth side. This wall was to be armed only along the parapet. Three-story brick barracks for the enlisted garrison paralleled the gunrooms on each flank. Of the 135 guns planned for the gunrooms and the open terreplein above, only 15 had been mounted. Most of these were "32 pounders"; none was heavier.

On December 20, 1860, South Carolina seceded from the Union. On the night of the 26th, fearing attack by the excited populace, Maj. Robert Anderson removed the small garrison he commanded at Fort Moultrie to Fort Sumter out in the harbor. He had two companies of the First United States Artillery —about 85 officers and men in a fortification intended for as many as 650. He had only "about 4 months" supply of provisions for his command. The question of reinforcement and supply was to trouble all the remaining days of the Buchanan administration and to carry over to the succeeding administration.

President Buchanan was persuaded to send off a relief expedition almost immediately. Initial plans called for the dispatch of the sloop of war *Brooklyn* for this purpose, but when word came which indicated that the South Carolinians had obstructed the harbor entrance by sinking several ships, it was decided to use an ordinary merchant ship. Accordingly, the *Star of the West*—a ship which regularly sailed southward from New York —was chartered. But Charleston was forewarned. When the *Star of the West* appeared at the entrance of the harbor on January 9, 1861, Citadel cadets opened fire with a gun mounted on Cummings Point; and the merchant ship unarmed, steamed out of the harbor. Anderson had held his fire and for the moment civil war had been averted.

Early in 1861, the Confederate Government was formed and in March President Lincoln took office. He was immediately faced with the Fort Sumter situation—lack of food and supplies. On April 4 Lincoln announced an expedition to supply Fort Sumter. It was the spark that set off the explosive forces which had been building up since

Damaged wall of Fort Sumter with howitzer used in repelling small-boat landing party of Union assault of 1864.

1850. The Confederate capital at Montgomery was informed. After cabinet debate in Montgomery, the Confederate Secretary of War ordered General Beauregard to demand the evacuation of the fort, and if that demand were refused, to "reduce it." On the afternoon of April 11, three of Beauregard's aides visited the fort under a flag of truce and presented the ultimatum. Major Anderson refused compliance, but at the same time he said, "Gentlemen, if you do not batter the fort to pieces about us, we shall be starved out in a few days."

Shortly after midnight, four Confederate officers confronted Major Anderson again. About 3 hours later, in a carefully worded reply, the Union commander agreed to evacuate "by noon on the 15th" unless he should receive prior to that time "controlling instructions from my Government or additional supplies." But it was expected in Charleston that the Federal supply ships would arrive before the 15th. Major Anderson's reply was rejected by the Confederate officers and orders given to open fire on Fort Sumter.

THE WAR BEGINS — APRIL 12, 1861

At 4:30 a.m., a mortar at Fort Johnson fired a shell which arched across the sky and burst almost directly over Fort Sumter. This was the signal for opening the bombardment. Within a few minutes, a ring of guns and mortars about the harbor—43 in all—were firing at Sumter.

Major Anderson withheld fire until about 7 o'clock. Then Capt. Abner Doubleday, of latter-day baseball fame, fired a shot at the Ironclad Battery on Cummings Point. Ominously, the light shot "bounded off from the sloping roof . . . without producing any apparent effect." Not at any time during the battle did the guns of Fort Sumter do great damage to the Confederate defenses. Most of Fort Sumter's heaviest guns were on the para-

Watercolor of the Battle of Fort Sumter painted by a slave known as Harley.

pet and in the parade, and, to reduce casualties in the small garrison, Major Anderson ordered these left unmanned. For a while, with the help of the 43 engineer workmen remaining at the fort, 9 or 10 of the casemate guns were manned. But by noon, the expenditure of ammunition was so much more rapid than the manufacture of new cartridge bags that the firing was restricted to 6 guns only. The barracks at Fort Sumter caught fire three times that first day, but each time the fire was extinguished. One gun on the parapet was dismounted; another damaged. When night descended, dark and stormy, Fort Sumter's fire ceased entirely. On the morning of the 13th, Sumter opened "early and spitefully," and, with the increased supply of cartridges, for a while kept up a brisk fire. About midmorning hot shot set fire to the officers' quarters. The blaze spread to the barracks. By noon the fort was almost uninhabitable.

About 1:30 in the afternoon the flag was shot down. Almost accidentally, this led to surrender. Col. Louis T. Wigfall, one of General Beauregard's aides, set out by small boat to ascertain whether Major Anderson would capitulate. He offered the Federal commander any terms he desired, only "the precise nature of which" would have to be arranged with General Beauregard. Anderson accepted on the basis of Beauregard's original terms: evacuation with his command, taking arms and all private and company property, saluting the United States flag as it was lowered, and being conveyed, if desired, to a Northern port. The white flag was raised and the firing ceased. About 7:30 that evening the engagement officially ended. During the 34-hour bombardment, more than 3,000 shells had been hurled at the fort.

On Sunday, April 14, Major Anderson and his garrison marched out of the fort with drums beating and colors flying and boarded ship to join the Federal fleet off the bar. On the 50th round of what was to have been a 100-gun salute to the United States flag, there occurred the only fatality of the engagement. The premature discharge of a gun and the explosion of a pile of cartridges resulted in the death of Pvt. Daniel Hough. Another wounded man died several days later.

The following day, April 15, 1861, Abraham Lincoln issued a call for 75,000 militia. Civil war, so long dreaded, had begun. The States of Virginia, Arkansas, Tennessee, and North Carolina now joined the Confederacy.

FEDERAL ATTEMPTS TO RETAKE SUMTER

With Fort Sumter in Confederate hands, the port of Charleston became a most irritating loophole in the Federal naval blockade of the Atlantic coast—doubly irritating because at Charleston "rebellion first lighted the flame of civil war."

In June 1862, an attempt was made by Maj. Gen. D. H. Hunter to push through to Charleston by James Island on the south. This ended in Union disaster at Secessionville. On April 5, 1863, a fleet of 9 Federal ironclads, armed with 32 guns "of the heaviest calibres ever used in war," appeared off Charleston bar. By 3 o'clock, the *Weehawken,* the leading monitor, had come within range, and Fort Moultrie opened fire. The *Passaic,* second in line, responded. Fort Sumter held fire, guns trained on a buoy at the turn of the channel. When the *Weehawken* came abreast of that point, all the guns atop Sumter's right flank let loose, followed by all the guns on Sullivan's Island, at Fort Moultrie, and at Cummings Point that could be brought to bear. It was too much for the ironclads. Five were disabled and one sunk. The Union attack had failed.

Federal authorities then looked to a combined sea-land operation to seize Morris Island and from there demolish Fort Sumter. With Fort Sumter reduced, the harbor could be entered. By July Federal batteries of heavy cannon were implaced in the marsh on Morris Island.

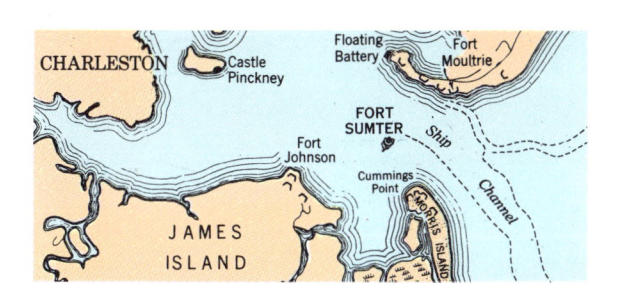

The bombardment of Fort Sumter began in earnest on August 17. A thousand shells were hurled at the fort that day; nearly 5,000 more during the week following. On the 21th, Brig. Gen. Quincy Gillmore of the Union land forces demanded the evacuation of Fort Sumter and Morris Island, threatening direct fire on the city of Charleston. Beauregard sent an indignant reply. By the 24th, General Gillmore was able to report the "practical demolition" of the fort. Still, the Confederate garrison, supplemented by a force of 200 to 400 Negroes, labored night and day, strengthening and repairing. The debris, accumulating above the sand-and cotton-filled rooms, itself bolstered the crumbling walls. General Beauregard ordered Fort Sumter held "to the last extremity." The bombardment continued sporadically for another week. Sumter remained defiant. When Admiral Dahlgren demanded the fort's surrender, on the morning of Sept. 7th, General Beauregard sent word that the admiral could have it when he could "take it and hold it." Dahlgren now determined upon a small-boat assault. The attack of the night of September 8-9 failed completely. Most of the boats never even reached the shore.

On October 26th the second great bombardment of the fort was started. The constant firing lasted until December when firing became intermittent and minor in character. The accumulation of rubble had made further bombardment ineffective. A stalemate was reached and on May 1, 1864, Gen. Gillmore left for Fort Monroe with 18,000 troops.

The third attempt to take Fort Sumter back was in the summer of 1864. Light-draft steamers and 1,000-man "assaulting arks" equipped with elevated towers for sharpshooters were used. The attack started in July, let up in August and finally ended in September. Sumter was still held by the Confederates, a symbol of resistance and courage for the entire South.

In February 1865, the long stalemate came to an end. In that month, General Sherman commenced his march north from Savannah through the interior of South Carolina, slicing between the remnants of Hood's army on the west and the small Confederate force remaining along the coast. On the 17th, with Sherman in Columbia, Fort Sumter and the other Confederate fortifications in Charleston harbor were quietly evacuated. At 9 o'clock on the morning of the 18th, the United States flag was once more raised over Fort Sumter. The fortunes of war had accomplished what 3,500 tons of metal, a fleet of ironclads, and thousands of men had failed to do.

On April 14, 1865, Robert Anderson, now a retired brigadier general, returned to Fort Sumter to raise again the flag he had pulled down 4 years before. The guns of the harbor thundered in salute.

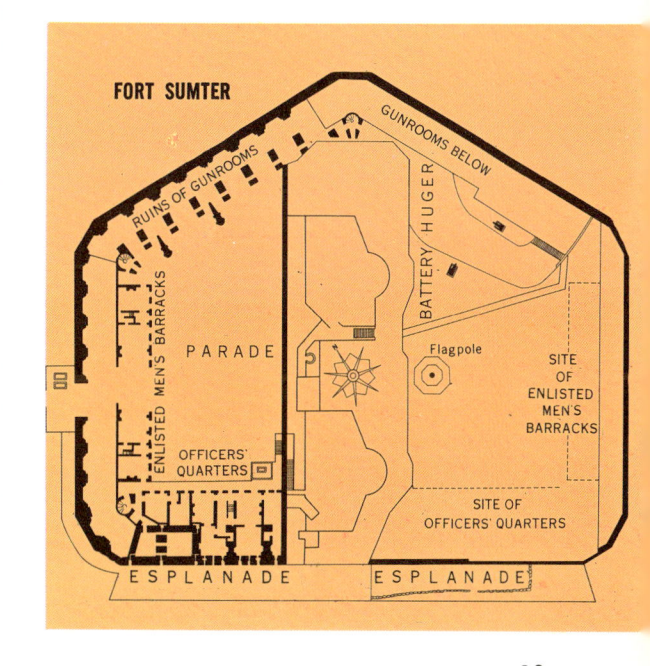

7 George Washington Birthplace

Westmoreland Co., Va.

The story of the Washington family plantation in Westmoreland County, Va., where George Washington was born on February 22, 1732, may be divided into 3 main parts. The first relates to the activities of the early Washingtons who lived on the plantation during the latter third of the 17th century and fourscore years of the 18th century — a period covering 115 years. During that time the plantation between Bridges Creek and Popes Creek grew; successive members of the Washington family became prosperous planters, and attained important civic and political offices in their county and colony. The climactic year of this first period was 1732 — when George, the son of Augustine and Mary Ball Washington, was born. The period ends during the American Revolution, when the home accidentally caught fire and burned to the ground.

The second period spans a hundred years— a century when the birthplace site was neglected, and was all but forgotten. Wild honeysuckle and bramble thickets covered the foundations of the burned home; the place was forgotten for so many years that knowledge of the exact location and use of many of the plantation buildings became lost.

The third and last period of the story covers the years when the Federal Government, various individuals, and patriotic organizations became interested in preserving the historic site; a period culminating in the preservation of the ancient plantation.

JOHN WASHINGTON

In late 1656, or early 1657, John Washington arrived in the Potomac River in Westmoreland County, Va., as mate of the ketch, *Sea Horse of London*. Owing to a disagree-

30

Opposite
Wakefield Memorial Mansion built in 1931 replaces the original Washington birthplace which burned in 1779.

ment with the owner and captain of the vessel John decided to remain in Virginia. A year or two after his arrival in Virginia, John married Anne Pope and, in 1659, was given land on Mattox Creek by his father-in-law, Col. Nathaniel Pope. Here their first son, Lawrence (George's grandfather), was born in September 1659.

On December 3, 1664, John Washington purchased from David Anderson 100 acres on the east side of Bridges Creek (only a short distance from its confluence with the Potomac River), and there he and Anne established their second home. Known as the Bridges Creek plantation, it was the first tract of land acquired by a Washington on the area which today is designated as George Washington Birthplace National Monument. The property later became a part of the plantation known as "Wakefield." John yearly added to his holdings, and at the time of his death owned several thousand acres of land in tidewater Virginia, including the property on the Potomac which later became known as Mount Vernon. John died in 1677 and was buried in the family cemetery at Bridges Creek.

LAWRENCE WASHINGTON

Lawrence Washington was 5 years old when his parents moved from Mattox Creek to the Bridges Creek plantation. In 1690 Lawrence married Mildred Warner of Gloucester County, Va., daughter of a prominent planter, Augustine Warner. Their second son, Augustine, born in 1694, was destined to become the father of George Washington. Lawrence Washington died in 1698, and was interred in the family cemetery at Bridges Creek.

AUGUSTINE WASHINGTON

George Washington's father, Augustine Washington, was born at Mattox Creek, Westmoreland County, Va., in 1694. He became of age in 1715, and shortly thereafter married Jane Butler, daughter of Caleb Butler, a successful Westmoreland County lawyer and planter. Four children were born of this union: Butler (who died in infancy), Lawrence (who built and named Mount Vernon), Augustine, Jr., and Jane.

In 1717-18 Augustine Washington bought from Joseph Abbington 150 acres of land on Popes Creek—a beautiful tract overlooking the tidal creek and the Potomac River. Some time between 1723 and 1725 Augustine Washington hired David Jones to build a house for him on his Popes Creek property. David Jones died in 1725 before the Washington house was completed. It may be inferred that the home was completed in 1726. While little is known about the appearance of the original home in which George Washington was born, the foundations and cellar floors uncovered during archeological excavations revealed that it was built either partially or entirely of brick.

The location of Augustine Washington's new home was superb, and must have been rather commodious, with furnishings and household items befitting a fairly large establishment. Certainly, the house in which George Washington was born could not have been the humble 1-story clapboard structure portrayed in 19th-century imaginative sketches by artists who probably knew little about the social and economic status of George Washington's father.

Though not a man of great wealth, Augustine imported fine quality silver, pewter, glassware, and pottery from the mother country, and could afford to have his monogram stamped on his wine bottles. He was a man of some influence in his community. He owned land and buildings in 3 Virginia counties. Jane Butler Washington died in 1729. Augustine married Mary Ball on March 6, 1731.

GEORGE WASHINGTON

On February 11 (Old Style), 1732, Mary Ball Washington gave birth to her first child, a boy she named George. The time was about 10 o'clock in the morning. The date, "11th Day of February," was "Old Style." By the Gregorian calendar, adopted by Great Britain in 1752 and now in use in the United States, the date was February 22, 1732, "New Style."

The first 3½ years of George's life were spent at the Popes Creek plantation. In 1742 Augustine acquired another tract of land between Popes Creek and Bridges Creek—within sight of the home where George was born. With the exception of one piece of property on the river all of the Popes Creek-Bridges Creek peninsula was now owned by George's father. In 1743 Augustine Washington died. Augustine left the Popes Creek-Bridges Creek plantation to his second son and namesake, Augustine, Jr.

After his father's death it appears that George stayed with his elder brother and sister-in-law on many occasions for long periods. George's elder half brother, Augustine Washington, Jr., died in 1762. The plantation passed to his son, William Augustine Washington, George's eldest nephew. About this time the Popes Creek plantation, for the first time, was called "Wakefield," a name said to have been inspired by Oliver Goldsmith's *Vicar of Wakefield,* and which has endured. During the latter part of the American Revolution, when General Washington was leading the Continental Army in the north, his birth home in faraway Virginia caught fire and burned to the ground. Indirect evidence and tradition indicate that the house was destroyed on Christmas Day, 1779. The home which had sheltered three generations of Washingtons for half a century was never rebuilt by them, and remained forgotten by Americans.

A CENTURY OF NEGLECT

After the disastrous fire at Wakefield, 36 years passed before the birthsite was marked. Finally, in 1815, George Washington Parke Custis (a grandson of Martha Washington and a ward of George Washington) visited Popes Creek and, in an imposing ceremony, marked what he considered to be the spot. Custis' visit to Washington's birthplace is important for two reasons. First, the freestone slab which he placed at the birthsite was one of the earliest monuments erected in the United States as a memorial to George Washington. Secondly, Custis describes the site as it appeared in 1815 as a "spot where a few scattered bricks alone marked the birthplace of the chief."

As the years passed during the 19th century, others who visited Washington's birthplace commented on the neglected condition of the site. In 1856 Lewis W. Washington offered to the State of Virginia "sixty feet square of ground on which the house stood in which General Washington was born" together with the family burying ground, provided "that the State shall cause the premises to be permanently enclosed by an iron fence, based on a stone foundation, and shall mark the same by suitable, and modest, though substantial tablets, to commemorate for the rising generation these notable spots." Gov. Wise was greatly interested in the offer, and as a result of his visit and recommendations, the Commonwealth of Virginia accepted the donation. Before the protective steps could be carried out, however, the Civil War broke out.

THE SAVING OF WASHINGTON'S BIRTHPLACE

The saving of Washington's Birthplace was the work of many individuals and organizations, the Commonwealth of Virginia, the Wakefield National Memorial Association, and the United States Government. In 1882 the Commonwealth of Virginia vested title

Dining room in the Wakefield Memorial Mansion.

in the United States of America to its holdings at the birthsite and burying ground. By an act of Congress approved in 1879, and amended in 1881, the construction of a monument to mark the birthsite and the acquisition of the necessary ground and right-of-way had been authorized. Although Congress had authorized the construction of a monument to mark the birthsite in 1881, 15 years passed before the shaft of Vermont granite was erected.

On February 23, 1923, the Wakefield National Memorial Association was organized. Their main objective was to restore the Wakefield plantation and make it a shrine for all people; the date set for completion of the task was 1932—the 200th anniversary of Washington's birth. Shortly after the Wakefield National Memorial Association was incorporated in 1924, its members raised funds for acquiring land between the birthsite and the Washington family burying ground, and induced John D. Rockefeller, Jr., to purchase 273 acres of the old Wakefield plantation and transfer it to the United States Government. By an act of Congress, approved June 7, 1926, the association was given authority to construct a house at Wakefield as nearly as possible like the one built by Augustine Washington. In 1929 the association acquired additional land, and 2 years later donated its holding at Wakefield (about 100 acres) to the United States.

By an act of Congress on January 23, 1930, the 394.47 acres owned by the Federal Government, was designated as George Washington Birthplace National Monument, to be administered by the National Park Service of the United States Department of the Interior. In 1930-31 the Wakefield National Memorial Association, under its authority from Congress, built an early 18th-century style brick home as a memorial to mark the approximate site of the home in which George Washington was born. The new memorial house was opened to the public in July 1931, and a special open house was held on February 22, 1932, the 200th anniversary of George Washington's birth. Since then the Wakefield National Memorial Association has been active in furnishing the home with suitable pieces of the 1700-50 period. In many instances 18-century artifacts unearthed near the site of the original home have served as guides in selecting certain items.

Since 1932 over a million people from all parts of the world have visited Wakefield and enjoyed its natural beauties and historical associations. But the restored plantation is more than a monument to the people who saved it and to the Americans who visit it. It is a memorial to the boy who played in the red brick house by the tidal creek. A boy who grew from youth into manhood and assumed greater responsibilities. The happy memories of days spent on his father's plantation were never forgotten.

8 Gettysburg Battlefield

Gettysburg, Pa.

Of the more than 2,000 land engagements of the Civil War, Gettysburg ranks supreme. Here at Gettysburg on July 1, 2, and 3, 1863, more men died than in any other battle fought before or since on North American soil. Here the Confederacy saw its greatest offensive turned back, saw its splendid army retreat to Virginia with no gain to match its valor and terrible sacrifices. Here for the first time in the war, the men in the Union Army of the Potomac rose up from their lines after the battle and cheered, aware that they had repulsed the hardest hammering that Robert E. Lee's Army of Northern Virginia could give them. Here—4 months later — President Lincoln summed up the meaning of the war, using 269 words that surpass the millions uttered and written since.

General Lee had led his men north of the Potomac River once before—in September 1862. He had hoped that a successful campaign on Northern soil might win foreign recognition for the Confederacy and lead to a negotiated peace. But the Battle of Antietam halted this invasion, and the war had continued.

Great Southern victories had since been won at Fredericksburg and Chancellorsville in Virginia. In the west, however, Union armies were probing deep into the Confederacy. The Southern stronghold at Vicksburg —key to control of the Mississippi River— was besieged. If Lee's veterans now launched another offensive across the Potomac, they might relieve the pressure on Vicksburg. Out of such hopes was born the Gettysburg Campaign.

The Army of Northern Virginia began its march on June 3. From Fredericksburg, where they had shielded Richmond from the Army of the Potomac, the long columns headed west through the gaps of the Blue Ridge, then northeast to Pennsylvania.

When Union Gen. Joseph Hooker saw the thin ranks Lee had left behind to screen Richmond, he wanted to strike for the Confederate Capital. But President Lincoln directed him to pursue Lee's army, keeping between the Southern host and Washington.

During Lee's northward march, his main body of cavalry under Gen. J.E.B. Stuart had swung to the east. Union forces in close pursuit cut Stuart off, depriving Lee of the "eyes" of his army. Lacking Stuart's reports, Lee did not know until June 28 that the Union army — now commanded by Gen. George G. Meade—was following him. Then, realizing that a battle was imminent, Lee ordered his scattered forces to concentrate at Cashtown, 8 miles west of Gettysburg.

Two days later, on June 30, Gen. John Buford's Union cavalry contacted a Confederate detachment near Gettysburg, then occupied McPherson Ridge. Now began the race to concentrate winning power.

THE FIRST DAY

Early on July 1, Buford's pickets opened fire on the Confederate vanguard approaching from Cashtown. Soon the Union cavalry was reinforced by Gen. John F. Reynolds' infantry. Dusty columns of both armies pounded toward the sound of the guns.

Until 1 p.m., the Union troops on McPherson Ridge held the attacking Confederates at bay. But suddenly the hills and ridges north of town came alive with charging men. In a concerted attack the powerful Confederate forces smashed into the Union lines.

Back through the town fled the men in blue. Many units fought heroic rearguard actions to protect their retreating comrades. By 5:30 p.m., the Union remnants were hurriedly entrenching south of Gettysburg on Cemetery Hill, where Gen. Winfield Scott Hancock—a rock in adversity—rallied their shattered ranks.

At the sound of the cannonade, General Lee had hastened to the front. He watched the Federals stream toward the hills south of town and begin their entrenchments. Though aware that their position was a strong one, he believed it could be crushed by attacking Culp's Hill or Cemetery Ridge.

THE SECOND DAY

By dawn, July 2, Lee's army was poised before the hook-shaped Union line; he hoped to break it before Meade's entire force reached the field. His plan of attack called for Gen. James Longstreet to assault the Union left on Cemetery Ridge. To aid the main attack, Gen. Richard Ewell's men would advance on Cemetery and Culp's Hills, at the right of the Union line.

Just after noon, Union Gen. Daniel Sickles pushed his troops westward from Cemetery Ridge. His new line formed a salient with its apex at the Peach Orchard on the Emmitsburg Road. This powerful intrusion further complicated Lee's attack plan.

Finally, at 4 p.m., Longstreet's batteries broke the silence. Gen. John B. Hood's division struck the Union flank at the Round Tops, Devil's Den, and the Wheatfield; close on his left, Lafayette McLaws' men charged the Union salient at the Peach Orchard. Farther north, R. H. Anderson's division struck the Emmitsburg Road. By sundown, the Confederates had completely shattered the Union salient.

But to the north, Ewell's attack on Cemetery and Culp's Hills had bogged down. Though individual units had been desperately brave, the attack failed for lack of coordination. Spangler's Spring and the Union works just north of it were captured after dark, but the main Union line stood unbroken. Except for the isolated struggle to the north, darkness ended the fighting and blotted from view the corpses that signified the day's work.

Though partially successful Lee had lost the race to win a decisive victory while still

35

holding the advantage of numbers. Throughout July 2, fresh infantry had filed into Meade's line and new batteries had wheeled into place. Facing Lee now, in a position growing ever stronger, was the entire Army of the Potomac.

THE THIRD DAY

July 3 broke with the thunder of Union guns near Spangler's Spring and Culp's Hill. After a struggle, the Federals recaptured the spring, erasing the threat to their right.

Meanwhile, Lee decided that further attacks against the strong Federal flanks were not feasible. To retain the initiative he decided upon a massive frontal assault against Meade's center.

His fighting blood up, Lee waved aside Longstreet's objections to a frontal assault against the strong Union line. Pointing to Cemetery Ridge, he exclaimed: "The enemy is there, and I am going to strike him."

Now Lee massed his forces along and in front of Seminary Ridge. J.E.B. Stuart—finally back with the army—began moving his cavalry to a point where he might harass the rear of the Federal army. (This design was thwarted when alert Union cavalry intercepted Stuart.)

Meanwhile, the Federal troops of General Hancock's Corps eyed the Confederate line from behind the stone wall that marked their position on Cemetery Ridge. A copse of trees provided shade for some of the men, but these lucky ones might have preferred the hot sun had they known that the Confederate attack was to be aimed directly at these trees.

At 1 o'clock, 140 Confederate guns in line from the Peach Orchard to the seminary let loose an earth-shaking cannonade. Federal artillery responded with counterbattery fire, and for a time the massed guns dueled for supremacy. Two hours later the cannonade died away.

General Longstreet ordered the advance and, with Gen. George Pickett's division on the right and those of James Pettigrew and Isaac Trimble on the left, nearly 15,000 Confederates moved forward.

The attackers now converged upon Meade's center. Momentarily the long lines were slowed by the rail fence at the Emmitsburg Road, then they rushed up the slope of Cemetery Ridge toward the line of fire erupting from the stone wall. From front and flank, double canister and rifle volleys assailed the charging line. They crumbled, re-formed, and again pressed forward.

Only 150 men led by Gen. Lewis Armistead crossed the stone wall, there to be overcome after savage hand-to-hand fighting. Meanwhile, Federal regiments to the right and to the left of The Angle wheeled in front of the stone wall and delivered a raking fire into the blunted wedge of Confederate attackers. A Union counter-charge swept the Confederates off Cemetery Ridge, and thousands of dead and wounded remained behind.

The remnant troops retreated toward the shelter of their guns. There General Lee told them to re-form, to rest, and to prepare defenses against a possible Federal attack.

Lee's supreme effort had failed. The Copse of Trees on Cemetery Ridge became the High Water Mark where the tide of the Confederacy had "swept to its crest, paused and receded." It was all over at Gettysburg.

Late on July 4, Lee began an orderly retreat southwest over the Hagerstown Road and through the mountain pass. Followed cautiously by Meade, Lee crossed the Potomac safely into Virginia on the night of July 13. The Army of Northern Virginia had escaped, but it had been so cruelly mauled that never again would it invade the North.

In the battle, 75,000 Confederates had been pitted against 97,000 Union troops. Lee lost 28,000 as against a Union loss of 23,000.

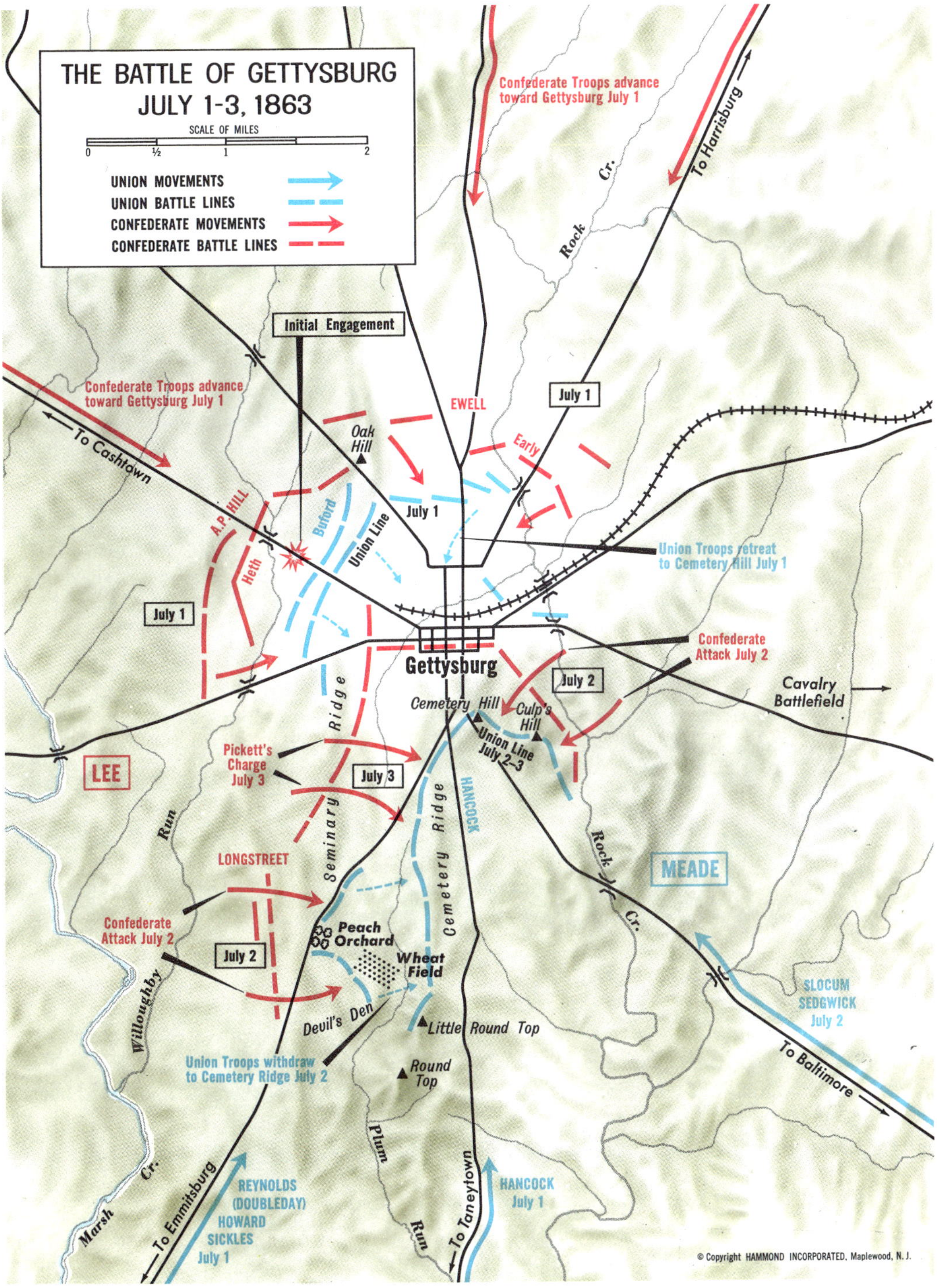
THE BATTLE OF GETTYSBURG
JULY 1-3, 1863
SCALE OF MILES
0
½
1
2
UNION MOVEMENTS
UNION BATTLE LINES
CONFEDERATE MOVEMENTS
CONFEDERATE BATTLE LINES
Confederate Troops advance toward Gettysburg July 1
To Harrisburg
Rock Cr.
Initial Engagement
Confederate Troops advance toward Gettysburg July 1
To Cashtown
EWELL
July 1
Oak Hill
Early
July 1
A.P. HILL
Buford
Union Line
Heth
Union Troops retreat to Cemetery Hill July 1
July 1
Gettysburg
Confederate Attack July 2
July 2
Cavalry Battlefield
Cemetery Hill
Culp's Hill
Ridge
Union Line July 2-3
Pickett's Charge July 3
July 3
LEE
HANCOCK
Run
Seminary
Cemetery Ridge
Rock Cr.
LONGSTREET
MEADE
Confederate Attack July 2
Peach Orchard
July 2
Wheat Field
Willoughby
Devil's Den
Little Round Top
SLOCUM SEDGWICK July 2
Union Troops withdraw to Cemetery Ridge July 2
Round Top
To Baltimore
Plum Run
Marsh Cr.
To Emmitsburg
REYNOLDS (DOUBLEDAY) HOWARD SICKLES July 1
To Taneytown
HANCOCK July 1
© Copyright HAMMOND INCORPORATED, Maplewood, N. J.

9
Golden Spike Historic Site

Promontory Point, Utah

At 12:47 p.m., May 10, 1869, the telegrapher's three dots—"DONE"—flashed coast to coast from Promontory Summit, Utah. The Golden Spike was driven, and rails from East and West were now connected. The Pacific railroad was a reality.

The greatest significance in the completion of the Pacific railroad was that it effected the first permanent breach in the far western frontier, set the pattern by which the frontier would be completely eliminated, and thus welded the Nation together.

RAILS FROM COAST TO COAST

The Golden Spike story began in the early 1830's—soon after the development of the locomotive—when men of vision first saw the immense benefits of a railroad from the Atlantic to the Pacific. But the reality of this dream was many years, many miles, many lives, and two wars away.

By the 1850's there was general agreement that without Federal help a Pacific railroad could not be built. But the issue of the eastern terminus remained unsettled.

FINANCING THE RAILROAD

The beginning of the Civil War ended the terminus and route debates. Spurred by the tireless lobbying of railroad promoters and by the urging of President Lincoln, Congress passed an acceptable Pacific railroad bill, and the President signed it on July 1, 1862. Under this act, the Central Pacific was to build from Sacramento eastward; the Union Pacific was to build from Omaha westward.

As generous as the terms of the railroad act were in subsidies and land grants, they proved inadequate to finance this gigantic undertaking. As a result, both companies indulged in shady financial manipulations. There was the inevitable reckoning. The financial methods pursued to build the Pacific resulted in inflated capitalization for both companies and meant decades of high rates and operating losses. The *Credit Mobilier* investigation in 1872 brought the railroads bad publicity. Almost all railroad historians agree that only through such methods could the railroad have been completed without far more liberal Government aid.

MEN AND MATERIALS

The Central Pacific broke ground in Sacramento in January 1863; the Union Pacific in Omaha in December 1863. Progress was slow until the Civil War ended. The CP had to ship at great expense all the equipment from the Atlantic coast around Cape Horn or across the Isthmus of Panama to San Francisco. The UP, until completion of the Chicago and Northwestern line to Council Bluffs in November 1867, drew its entire stock of materials from Missouri River steamers. All material and supplies for the army of workers then had to be forwarded by train from the terminus to end-of-track. Beyond end-of-track the grading crews and surveying parties had to be supplied by wagon train.

Until the end of the Civil War, materials and manpower were in short supply. Then war veterans, mostly Irish immigrants, flocked to Omaha to join UP's construction crews. The CP had a more serious manpower problem. Railroad wages failed to lure men from the goldfields. The CP imported Chinese laborers to build its road.

BUILDING THE RAILROAD

The towering Sierra Nevada presented enormous engineering obstacles and strangling winter snows to the Central Pacific. The Union Pacific encountered little difficult terrain until it reached central Wyoming and Utah. Though the terrain was easy, UP had a problem not experienced by CP — Indians. The Army and the railroad workers had to fight many skirmishes as the rails pushed westward.

Completion of the Pacific railroad, May 10, 1869. The artist's painting below shows the last spike being driven at Promontory Summit, Utah Territory.

THE GREAT RAILROAD RACE

By mid-1868 the great railroad race was in full swing. The intent of Congress was that the two companies were to build until they met. This junction point was never spelled out in the laws. This meant that both builders tried to lay as much track as possible to capture the territory before the opposition got it. In April 1869, representatives of the two companies met in Washington and chose Ogden, Utah, as the final junction point. The actual joining of the rails would be at Promontory Summit.

DRIVING THE GOLDEN SPIKE

May 8 was chosen as the date for joining the rails, but delays set it back 2 days. On May 10, the UP delegation arrived. It was headed by Dr. Thomas Durant, vice-president. The CP delegation and its president, Leland Stanford, had arrived 3 days earlier. Ceremonies began at noon. Construction superintendents for the CP and UP slid a polished laurel tie, predrilled to receive four ceremonial spikes, under the rails at 12:20. After opening remarks and a prayer, Dr. Durant standing at the west rail received two gold spikes from California and dropped them into the tie. Stanford placed a silver spike from Nevada and a spike of an alloy of iron, gold, and silver from Arizona into their holes. Then these spikes were symbolically "driven" with a silver-plated sledge. Finally came the actual driving of the last spike. The sledge was wired and connected to the UP telegraph. Both Stanford and Durant took a swing at the spike and missed. Nevertheless the telegrapher tapped out "DONE" and triggered celebrations in every major city in the Nation.

The Central Pacific's *Jupiter* backed up and the Union Pacific's *119* crossed the junction onto the CP tracks. Then *119* backed up and *Jupiter* crossed onto the UP tracks. Thus transcontinental rail travel was symbolized. A golden spike had introduced a golden era.

10
Independence Hall

Philadelphia, Pa.

Independence Hall was originally the State House of Pennsylvania. For a half century after the establishment of the Province, the government had no official building. In order to meet the needs of the Province, funds were appropriated for the construction of the State House in 1729. Strong disagreement arose as to the location and plan. This disagreement delayed actually beginning work on the building until 1732. In that year the Assembly approved the plan Andrew Hamilton advocated and selected the south side of Chestnut Street between Fifth and Sixth Streets as the site. This was then on the outskirts of the city.

In the 1730's, Philadelphia had a population of almost 11,500 people. Only Boston, with 13,000, was larger; while New York was third, with 8,500. The area of what was to become Independence Square contained only a few small houses.

It is apparent that the plans from which the State House was constructed were drawn by Edmund Woolley, master carpenter, who was also the principal builder under the direction of Andrew Hamilton. To these two men go the major credit for the design and erection of one of the most beautiful administrative buildings of the Colonial period.

Building the State House was a slow process. Difficulties of various kinds, especially the scarcity of skilled workmen, kept the building in an unfinished state until 1748.

Although the 15 years required to build the State House must have been a source of irritation to legislators eager to occupy it, the completed building proved the time was well spent. A most ambitious project for that early date, it emerged a sturdily constructed brick edifice—described at the time as a "large handsome building"—with a facade 107 feet in length connected by closed arcades, or "piazzas," to wing buildings some 50 feet long. The main building had a decked gable roof, balustraded between the chimneys and surmounted by a centrally located cupola. The interior arrangement of the State House provided suitable space for the various agencies of government. The first floor contained two chambers about 40 feet square, separated by a spacious center hall about 20 feet wide. The eastern chamber served as the meeting place of the Assembly. This room, in the words of a contemporary in 1774, was "finished in a neat but not elegant manner."

It is apparent that the State House was not elegantly furnished. Chairs, tables, curtains, screens, and other items purchased for the building were never unduly expensive. However, the silver inkstand, purchased from Philip Syng, of Philadelphia, for the table of the Speaker of the Assembly, and still preserved in Independence Hall, was a most unusual item which cost £25-16-0. The building appears to have been heated originally by open fireplaces for which stoves were later substituted. Lighting was not a serious problem since the meetings rarely continued until darkness; when they did, the Assembly ordered that candles be brought in.

In January 1750, shortly after the State House was completed, the Assembly authorized the superintendents of the building to erect a tower to contain a staircase and belfry. Edmund Woolley was entrusted with the construction. By 1753, the tower was completed and the State House bell (now called the Liberty Bell), ordered in 1751, was hung. The Assembly also ordered a "large Clock to strike on the Bell."

THE STATE HOUSE AND INDEPENDENCE

Philadelphia, the metropolis of English America, was destined to become even more prominent during the American Revolution. As opposition to England's colonial policy developed in America, the city's location near the center of colonial America naturally made it the focal point of government. In

September 1774 the Americans chose representatives to an intercolonial congress which was to become known as the First Continental Congress. This body met at Carpenters' Hall in Philadelphia to plot a course of action in the dispute with England.

Although the First Continental Congress protested strongly against violations of the "rights of Englishmen" claimed for the American colonists, no demand for independence was made.

After the first Congress adjourned on October 26, 1774, relations between the colonies and the mother country grew steadily worse. On April 19, 1775, the Minute Men of Massachusetts fought the British forces at Lexington and Concord. About a month later, on May 10, the Second Continental Congress met in an atmosphere of tension in the Assembly Room of the State House. The governing body, forced by events, moved from protest to resistance.

On June 7, 1776, Richard Henry Lee of Virginia offered a resolution declaring, "That these United Colonies are, and of right ought to be, free and independent States," and that foreign alliances and a plan of confederation ought to be created. A committee, composed of Thomas Jefferson, John Adams, Benjamin Franklin, Roger Sherman, and Robert R. Livingston, was named to draft a declaration "setting forth the causes which impelled us to this mighty resolution."

On July 2, 1776, Lee's resolution was adopted after a heated debate. Two days later, the Congress formalized this act by adopting the Declaration of Independence. On August 2, after it had been engrossed, the document was signed by most members of Congress. These drastic and irrevocable actions marked the end of British rule and the birth of the United States of America.

Throughout the many and hard years of the Revolution, the Congress sat in the State

41

View of the Assembly Room where the Declaration of Independence was signed.

House, except for periods of danger such as the occupation of Philadelphia by the British forces from September 1777 to June 1778. The occupation of Philadelphia by the British had been a period of distress not only for the American cause but for the State House as well. The building had first been used as quarters for British troops. After the battle of Germantown, it served as a hospital for wounded American soldiers.

These uses of the building had left it, in the words of a member of the Congress, in "a most filthy and sordid situation," with "the inside torn much to pieces." Extensive cleaning and repairs were required to refit the building for the State Government and the Congress.

The Revolutionary period also saw an alteration on the exterior of the State House—the removal of the badly decayed wooden steeple above the brick tower. The Assembly considered this step as early as 1773, but the project was not carried out until 1781. After the steeple was removed, the brick tower was covered with a low, sloping, hipped roof, surmounted by a slender finial.

In 1783, a body of mutinous soldiers surrounded the State House and demanded back pay from Congress. Although the members of Congress were unharmed, the incident led to their moving to Princeton. A time of discontent had come and the search for a stronger central government began. As a result, Congress called a convention to amend the Articles of Confederation. The Federal Constitutional Convention opened in Philadelphia on May 25, 1787, in the same room in the State House where the Declaration of Independence had been adopted.

The Convention, composed of 55 men chosen by the legislatures of the States, was a small group, but included the best minds in America.

Throughout the hot summer months, the delegates presided over by George Washington labored. The Constitution was not born at once, but developed gradually through debate, interchange of opinion, and careful consideration of problems. Many minds contributed to its final form; James Madison was in many ways the most effective, followed by James Wilson.

On September 17, 1787, 4 months after the Convention had assembled, the finished Constitution was signed. When the Constitution was finally ratified, the Congress arranged for the first national election.

The new Federal Government first began its work in New York. In 1790, the Government came to Philadelphia and remained there for 10 years.

AFTER 1800

With the turn of the century, Philadelphia ceased to be a capital city. In 1800, the Federal Government moved to Washington. During the previous year, the State Government had moved first to Lancaster and later to Harrisburg. The State House became an empty building, used apparently only at elections. The building and land were offered for sale by the State Government. The City of Philadelphia purchased the building and

Two centuries of time have brought changes in the appearance of Independence Hall. Since 1898, however, modifications have been slight.

square for the sum of $70,000. The City took title on March 23, 1818. This was a financial and spiritual investment unequaled in the history of American cities.

Although the City of Philadelphia had saved the State House and its sister buildings from possible destruction, it was evident that many did not consider the ensemble worthy of complete preservation. The old wings and the committee room of the State House were demolished, to be replaced by "modern" office buildings designed by the architect, Robert Mills. These new offices consisted of two row buildings attached to the east and west ends of the State House. Often called "State House row," they were occupied by various officials of the city, county, and federal governments. Other changes followed. The Assembly Room, in which the Declaration of Independence had been adopted, was converted into a court room. This was "modernized" by the removal of its paneling and the substitution of plaster and paint.

The first occupant after the State government moved was Charles Willson Peale, who, in 1802, received permission to use the upper floor of the State House (including the tower rooms) and the Assembly Room on the first floor, for his museum which had occupied Philosophical Hall since 1794. This museum remained in the State House until 1828. By the terms of the agreement, Peale was responsible for the maintenance of both the building and the State House Yard. He planted trees, added new gates and benches, and improved the walls and lawns. It was most fortunate that a man of Peale's caliber was responsible for the property's care during this dark period.

EVOLUTION OF A SHRINE

The "State House" did not become "Independence Hall" till the last half of the 19th century. This change in designation, which began about the time of Lafayette's visit to America, is closely linked with the evolution of the building as a national shrine.

Prior to 1824, there was but little reverence or regard for the State House. The visit of the Marquis de Lafayette to Philadelphia in that year, however, awakened an interest in the building which has persisted to this day.

Lafayette was formally received in the "Hall of Independence" by the Mayor and other dignitaries on September 28. On the days following, during his week-long visit, the chamber served as his levee room.

The interest in the State House engendered by Lafayette's visit was not permitted to die. In 1828, the City Councils obtained plans and estimates to rebuild the wooden steeple which had been removed in 1781. After heated discussions, William Strickland's design for the new steeple was accepted, a large bell to be cast by John Wilbank was ordered, and Isaiah Lukens was commissioned to construct a clock. Work was completed on the project during the summer of 1828.

In the 1850's, and during the critical years of the Civil War, veneration for the State House became even more evident. In 1852, the Councils resolved to celebrate July 4 annually "in the said State House, known as Independence Hall. . . ." This is the first clear-cut use of the term "Independence Hall" to designate the entire building.

Perhaps the best expression of this veneration is in the grandiloquent words of the famed orator Edward Everett, who, on July 4, 1858, said of the State House, or as it has now come to be known, Independence Hall: "Let the rain of heaven distill gently on its roof and the storms of winter beat softly on its door. As each successive generation of those who have benefitted by the great Declaration made within it shall make their pilgrimage to that shrine, may they not think it unseemly to call its walls Salvation and its gates Praise."

THE STORY OF A SYMBOL

The Liberty Bell is the most venerated symbol of patriotism in the United States; its fame as an emblem of liberty is worldwide. In the affections of the American people today it overshadows even Independence Hall, although veneration for the latter began much earlier. Its history, a combination of facts and folklore, has firmly established the Liberty Bell as the tangible image of political freedom. The known facts about the Liberty Bell can be quickly told. Properly, the story starts on November 1, 1751, when the superintendents of the State House of the Province of Pennsylvania (now Independence Hall) ordered a "bell of about two thousand pounds weight" for use in that building.

It was stipulated that the bell should have cast around its crown the Old Testament quotation, "Proclaim liberty throughout all the land, unto all the inhabitants thereof." Most likely, this phrase was chosen in commemoration of William Penn's Charter of Privileges issued 50 years earlier.

Thomas Lester's foundry at Whitechapel, in London, was the scene of casting the bell. Soon after its arrival in Philadelphia, in August 1752, the brand new bell was cracked "by a stroke of the clapper without any other violence as it was hung up to try the sound."

By 1753, the bell was repaired and began its period of service, summoning the legislators to the Assembly and opening the courts of justice in the State House.

With the threat of British occupation of Philadelphia in 1777, the State House bell and other bells were hastily moved from the City to prevent their falling into British hands and being made into cannon. Taken to Allentown, the bell remained hidden under the floor of the Zion Reformed Church for almost a year. In the summer of 1778, upon the withdrawal of the British, it was deemed safe to return the bells to Philadelphia.

The words "Proclaim liberty throughout the land..." inscribed on the Liberty Bell were chosen 25 years earlier from the Bible, Leviticus 25:10.

By 1773, the State House steeple had become so dangerously weakened that it was removed in 1781 and the bell lowered into the brick tower. Some 50 years later, in 1828, when the wooden steeple was rebuilt, a new and larger bell was acquired. The old bell, almost forgotten, probably remained in the tower. The new one was obtained, perhaps, because the original had either cracked or had shown indications of cracking. Traditionally, the fracture occurred while the bell was being tolled during the funeral procession of Chief Justice John Marshall some 7 years later. In 1846, an attempt was made to restore the bell's tone by drilling the crack so as to separate the sides of the fracture. This attempt failed. The bell was actually tolled for Washington's birthday, but for the last time, for the crack began to spread.

Now that the bell was mute, useless as a summoner or sounder of alarms, it began to assume a new and more vital role. Over the years it came to be a symbol of human liberty—a very substantial symbol of 2,080 pounds of cast metal—inscribed with the Biblical admonition to "proclaim liberty."

It is difficult to find the exact beginnings of this veneration for the Liberty Bell. Independence Hall, the building with which it is so intimately associated, began its evolution as a patriotic shrine about the time of Lafayette's visit in 1824, but the bell, rarely mentioned earlier, still received no notice.

Probably the first use of the bell as a symbolic device dates from 1839. In that year, some unknown person apparently noted the forgotten inscription on the bell. This was immediately seized upon by adherents of the antislavery movement who published a pamphlet, entitled *The Liberty Bell*. This is also the first known use of that name. Previously, the bell was called the Old State House Bell, the Bell of the Revolution, or Old Independence. That publication was followed by others which displayed the bell, greatly idealized, as a frontispiece. Thus the bell became identified with early antislavery propaganda, invoking the inscription of a promise of freedom to "all the inhabitants." During this time, it is interesting to note, the symbolism of the bell served a narrow field; little, if any, thought was given it as a patriotic relic.

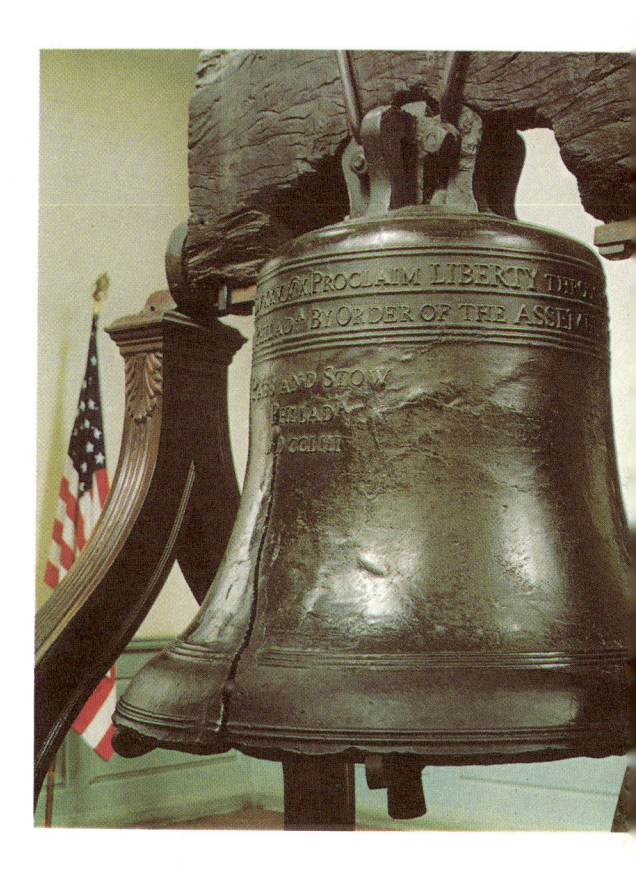

But patriotism was the next logical step. In the first half of the 19th century the bell became the subject of legendary tales which it has not been possible to verify. These legends have been recited in prose and poetry; they have found their way into children's textbooks; and they have contributed greatly to rousing the patriotic enthusiasm of succeeding generations of Americans.

45

11
Jamestown

Jamestown, Va.

The first permanent settlement in America by the English was proof of their determination to establish themselves in the New World. The defeat of Spanish sea power by the English during the reign of Queen Elizabeth had paved the way for English colonization of America. Enterprising Britons had already established their influence in India, the Near East, and Russia. Sir Walter Raleigh had made several unsuccessful attempts to establish an enduring settlement along the Carolina coast at Roanoke Island. It remained for the Virginia Company of London, under its charter of April 10, 1606, to found the first permanent English settlement in America. Jamestown is the site of this settlement.

The first settlers landed in May 1607, built houses and a fort, planted crops; and began the struggle for the conquest of the continent. They brought with them their Church and respect for God. They established homes, maintained trial by jury and their rights as free men, and soon they were developing representative government, intent upon the realization of Raleigh's dream of a great English nation beyond the seas.

17TH CENTURY JAMESTOWN

The story of Jamestown began on May 13, 1607, when the first Virginia colonists, after several months of voyaging out of England and a brief stay on Cape Henry, sailed up

Opposite
Costumed pageantry amid authentic reproductions of 17th century buildings at Jamestown.

the James River and selected Jamestown Island, then a peninsula, as a place for settlement. They disembarked from their three small ships, the *Susan Constant,* the *Godspeed,* and the *Discovery,* on the following day. Virginia was a pleasant land, but its ways were strange to Englishmen, and the first years at Jamestown were trying ones —a continual struggle against sickness, hunger, and inexperience, in addition to the disadvantages of its unhealthful location.

Within a few months Captain John Smith became the dominant personality at Jamestown. His vigorous leadership did much to keep the Colony together during its first two and one-half years. His departure for England in October 1609, seemingly under duress and after he had been disabled by an explosion of gunpowder, marked the beginning of the terrible "Starving Time," when nine-tenths of the colonists died. Discouragement was so great that the survivors planned to desert the Colony. It was only the timely arrival of the newly appointed governor, Lord Delaware, with fresh men and supplies, that actually prevented the abandonment of Virginia.

Gradually, Jamestown took on a look of permanence, and plantations spread up and down the rivers. By 1614, the settlement could boast of streets and houses and could well be called a town.

The efficient, yet necessarily stern, government of Sir Thomas Dale did much to stabilize the Colony, particularly through his assignment of private holdings and his rigid enforcement of a stringent disciplinary code of laws. About 1610-11, experimentation in tobacco culture, ably advanced by John Rolfe, proved successful. This established the economic basis on which the Colony became prosperous.

In 1614, Pocahontas, the daughter of the Indian Chieftain Powhatan, married John Rolfe, bringing 8 years of peace with the Indians. Two years later, in 1616, she went to England and was presented to the Court of James I as Lady Rebecca. She died in England in 1617 leaving a son, Thomas Rolfe, who later came to Virginia and left many descendants.

The year 1619 was truly a momentous one for the Colony. Maids arrived from England to become wives of the settlers and to join with those of their sex already in Virginia. In this year, too, the first Negroes were brought to the Colony. More significant still was the meeting of the House of Burgesses, which convened in the church at Jamestown in what was the first representative legislative assembly in the New World.

In the year 1622, there was a sudden uprising of the Indians which resulted in wholesale destruction of life and property. Jamestown, warned through the friendly Indian, Chanco, escaped the massacre, though for a time the whole life of the Colony was threatened. Partly as a result of these events, the Virginia Company of London, which had directed the affairs of the settlement since its founding, was dissolved, and Virginia became a royal colony in 1624.

The Virginians, though as yet loyal to the British sovereign, were increasingly conscious of their strength and jealous of their rights. Under the administration of Sir William Berkeley, popular feeling against personal government mounted for a time to the pitch of open rebellion as a result of his high-handed acts, and of Indian depredations on the frontier. In 1676, Nathaniel Bacon, the younger, emerged as the popular leader in a revolt which brought hostilities to Jamestown and momentarily drove Berkeley from power. Bacon's men burned the town, believing it to be the "stronghold of oppression."

Bacon soon died, and the rebellion collapsed, leaving, however, an undying spirit of resistance to tyranny. Berkeley was re-

The Old Church Tower built in 1639 is all that is left of 17th century Jamestown.

placed, and Jamestown was partially rebuilt; but the town had suffered a blow from which it never quite recovered. The burning of the statehouse in 1698 brought the end. The seat of government was moved to Williamsburg in 1699, and, before many years had passed, Jamestown was practically abandoned. The town ceased to exist about the time of the American Revolution. At about this time, too, the isthmus connecting Jamestown to the mainland was washed out, making it a true island.

POINTS OF INTEREST AT JAMESTOWN

The principal area of the town of Jamestown, which grew out of the settlement in 1607, was along the James River on both sides of, and including, the present highway. It was approximately three-fourths of a mile long and extended from the river back to the salty marsh, called Pitch and Tar Swamp. At first there was only the fort. Then, as the town grew, there were houses, a church, a market place, shops, storehouses, statehouses, and other public buildings along regularly laid out streets and ways. This was the capital of Virginia until 1699.

The *first landing site,* which the colonists reached on May 13, 1607, and where, the next day, they landed supplies, has been fixed by tradition as a point now in the river approximately 125 feet from the present sea wall, almost directly out from the Old Church Tower. The *first fort,* triangular in shape, by tradition was located in front of the Tower and likewise on land that has been washed away by the James River.

The ivy-covered *Old Church Tower* is the only standing ruin of the seventeenth century town of Jamestown. It is believed to have been constructed as a part of the first brick church, begun in 1639. The walls of handmade brick, 3 feet thick, laid in English bond, have been standing for more than 300 years. The *Memorial Church,* adjoining the Tower, was erected in 1907 by the Colonial Dames of America over the foundations of this early brick church. Within the building are burials, memorials, and the foundations of an earlier church said to have housed the first representative legislative assembly in America which convened on July 30, 1619. In the *Churchyard* countless dead are buried and the few remaining gravestones are witness to the antiquity of the spot. These carry the names of Berkeley, Blair, Harrison, Ludwell, Beverley, Lee, and others.

Northwest of the Church area is a group of excavated foundations of buildings of importance in the later years of the town of Jamestown. These include the *Last Statehouse,* the *Last Country House,* and three houses of Philip Ludwell. Erosion has taken at least 25 acres of the northern portion of the town site. Through the efforts of the Association for the Preservation of Virginia Antiquities, the

Replicas of the Susan Constant, Godspeed, *and* Discovery *which landed at Jamestown.*

United States, in 1900-01, built a concrete sea wall to check further damage. Col. Samuel H. Yonge, author of *The Site of Old "James Towne,"* was the engineer in charge. This sea wall and the riprap extension later provided by the National Park Service now protect the Island from further erosion.

In "New Towne" where Jamestown expanded about 1620 lived many of the principal figures of early Virginia. The *Country House,* the foundations of which have been located, was used by the governor as his residence. In it lived Governors Sir Samuel Argall, Sir George Yeardley, and Sir Francis Wyatt. In this section were the residences of Richard Kemp, builder of the first recorded brick house in Virginia; Dr. John Pott and William Pierce, leaders in "the thrusting out" of Gov. John Harvey in 1635; and William Sherwood, an attorney general for the Colony. Here have been excavated the foundations of the house of *Henry Hartwell,* one of the founders of the College of William and Mary.

Near the river the foundations of the *First Brick Statehouse* of Virginia have been discovered. Here, during the early governorship of Sir William Berkeley, were discussed the measures needful for the government of the growing colony. Here, too, the Colony submitted to the government of the Commonwealth of England in 1652, and Richard Bennett, chosen by the Assembly, succeeded Berkeley as governor.

The *Tercentenary Monument* erected by the United States in 1907 commemorates the 300th anniversary of the settlement. Built of New Hampshire granite, it rises 103 feet above its base. Other monuments and memorials, all of which are within the APVA Grounds, include the *Captain John Smith Statue* designed by William Couper; the *Pocahontas Monument,* by William Ordway Partridge; the *House of Burgesses Monument,* listing the members of the first representative legislative body in the New World; and the *Memorial to the Reverend Robert Hunt,* who in June 1607, on the third Sunday after Trinity, administered at Jamestown the first Holy Communion according to the rites of the Church of England.

The ruined walls of the *Jaquelin-Ambler House* stand as testimony of the late colonial period when Jamestown Island ceased to be the location of a town and became the estate of two families—Ambler and Travis. A reminder of a later period is the *Confederate Fort,* near the Old Church Tower, built in 1861. This is one of several such fortifications on the Island.

Jamestown Island, except Jamestown National Historic Site, is in Colonial National Historical Park. The park also includes Yorktown Battlefield, Colonial Parkway, and Cape Henry Memorial. Jamestown National Historic Site is administered by the Association for the Preservation of Virginia Antiquities.

12
Jefferson National Expansion Memorial

St. Louis, Mo.

When the Thirteen Original States gained their independence in 1783, the western boundary of the new Nation was established at midstream of the Mississippi, from its source to near Natchez, Miss. Only a few trailblazers and settlers had crossed the Appalachians at that time, but soon mounting numbers of land-hungry pioneers began to fill this region. Floating down the Ohio River or trudging through Cumberland Gap on the Wilderness Road, they filtered into the Old Northwest and into Kentucky and Tennessee. By 1800 they had reached the banks of the Mississippi River.

The vision of President Thomas Jefferson, the great architect of westward expansion, led to the purchase of the vast French empire of Louisiana from Napoleon in 1803. This brilliant act doubled the land area of the infant republic and assured the United States of a major role in the settlement of the North American continent. The West was not to be preserved for Old World empires. It was to be a rich land of opportunity for Americans.

The annals of the West include the pageant of exploration and the fur trade; covered wagon migrations; the Pony Express and the transcontinental telegraph; stage, freight, and railroad lines; steamboats churning western rivers; cowboys and a range empire of grass; the last phase of Indian warfare; courageous homesteaders; boomtowns, and new States in the Union.

GATEWAY TO THE WEST

Founded in 1764 by French fur traders from New Orleans, St. Louis slowly grew to be an outpost of French-Canadian culture and a governmental center of imperial Spain. In 1803 the city became part of the United States through the Louisiana Purchase.

Its strategic location on a flood-free bluff, convenient to the Ohio, Missouri, and other river approaches, made St. Louis the hub of midcontinental commerce, transportation, and culture, and a gateway to the wilderness beyond.

It was the headquarters of the western fur trade. Manuel Lisa, the Chouteaus, Ashley, Sublette, and other leaders of the trade built their homes here and directed the activities of the legendary mountain men. Along the riverfront, towering steamboats from the East and South met the smaller riverboats serving the frontier communities and outposts on the upper Mississippi and Missouri Rivers.

Opposite
Gateway Arch of stainless steel frames St. Louis' Old Cathedral.

Right
The Old Courthouse at the Memorial site.

Restless pioneers, congregating at this settlement before starting out across the plains, purchased supplies and outfits, then boarded steamboats which took them 400 miles up the Missouri to the river bend at the Kansas border. Here, where the Missouri turns north, the frontier towns of Westport and Independence sprang up. Thousands of wagons which rolled to Santa Fe, Oregon, and California were moved by steamboat from St. Louis.

This stretch of riverfront remained the supply base and marketplace of the frontier for many years. Oregon pioneers and gold seekers bought tools, wagons, guns, and supplies here, and lumbermen, planters, farmers, and fur traders sold their products. Goods were manufactured here too: Newell & Sutton plows, Murphy wagons for the Santa Fe trade, Grimsley dragoon saddles, Hawken "plains" rifles, and the cast-iron stoves of Filley and Bridge & Beach.

The business center of old St. Louis grew up along the levee. But when the Eads Bridge was completed in 1874 and the railroad came of age, business moved uptown, the riverfront declined, and the historic buildings gradually disappeared. Only two — the Old Courthouse and the Old Cathedral — still stand within the memorial.

THE MEMORIAL CONCEPT

This memorial was established in 1935 as a testament to Thomas Jefferson and others who directed the territorial expansion of the United States to the Pacific and to recount the exploits of those who explored and occupied the American West.

To dramatize this growth and the great social, political, and economic changes that followed in the wake of the Louisiana Purchase, the National Park Service and the city of St. Louis have undertaken an extensive development program along the riverfront. In 1947 the Jefferson National Expansion Memorial Association, a group of citizens interested in this work, held a national competition to select a suitable design for the memorial. The Gateway Arch, submitted by the late Eero Saarinen, was chosen.

The central feature of the Saarinen plan — one filled with architectural innovation—is the soaring stainless steel arch, symbolic of St. Louis' historic role. One of the most challenging engineering and construction projects ever tackled, the arch rises to 630 feet —75 feet higher than the Washington Monument. In section, the arch is an equilateral triangle, 54 feet on a side at the base, tapering to about 17 feet at the top. A capsule transporter in each leg whisks visitors to the observation platform at the top.

The Old Courthouse, high above the river on the western edge of the old business district, was the focal point of the community when St. Louis was the "Emporium of the West." It was begun in 1839 to replace an outgrown smaller brick structure and completed in 1864, after many changes in the original plans. Carl Wimar's historical and allegorical murals—now restored—decorate the rotunda. The building was a public forum as well as a courthouse. Here the community honored its volunteers returning from the Mexican War; a national convention met to project a railroad to the Pacific; Senator Thomas Hart Benton delivered his famous oration, using as his theme Bishop Berkeley's phrase, "Westward the course of empire"; and the slave Dred Scott sued for his freedom and in a decade of litigation focused national attention anew on the slavery controversy.

The Old Cathedral, adjacent to the memorial, was built between 1831 and 1834 on land set aside for religious purposes when St. Louis was founded. The only structure standing on its original foundations in old St. Louis, it narrowly escaped destruction in the disastrous fire of 1849.

13
Lincoln Memorial

Washington, D.C.

This memorial honors the virtues of tolerance, honesty, and constancy in the human spirit. The man whose likeness presides over this marbled hall used these virtues in the practice of statecraft. And from it flowed everlasting benefit to his nation and an enduring inspiration to his countrymen.

Had Lincoln been an ordinary president—even an ordinary hero—an ordinary monument would have sufficed and no doubt would have been quickly built. More than half a century elapsed, however, before an appropriate memorial to the man arose in the Nation's Capital. It seemed as if time stood aside until coming generations could fashion the perfect tribute to their benefactor. The memorial is neither temple, palace, nor tomb, but partakes something of all. It seems to gather within its marble walls the spirit of the man's character, his belief that all people should be free, free to think and express themselves, and free to apply their natural talents and ambitions in lawful enterprise.

BUILDING THE MEMORIAL

The first organized effort to erect a monument to Lincoln in Washington occurred 2 years after his death. An act of Congress approved March 29, 1867, incorporated the Lincoln Monument Association. The association appealed for subscriptions and prepared plans for a monument. But there was no practical accomplishment from this effort. The years passed. Although numerous subsequent efforts were made to secure a memorial, it was not until February 1911 that Congress passed the legislation that procured it. In that act, Congress provided for a "Commission to secure plans and designs for a Monument or Memorial to the memory of Abraham Lincoln."

The commission held its first meeting on March 4, 1911. Almost a year later, at its 10th meeting on February 3, 1912, it decided to locate the memorial in Potomac Park on the axis of the Capitol and the Washington Monument, facing east toward them. This site had been recommended by the Commission of Fine Arts. Upon invitation, Henry Bacon and John Russell Pope, architects of New York City, prepared designs for a structure. The commission selected Henry Bacon to prepare a final design, and Congress approved this on January 29, 1913.

Workmen broke ground at the site selected for the memorial on February 12, 1914. The cornerstone was laid a year later. As work progressed on the structure, the commission selected Daniel Chester French to sculpture the Lincoln statue and Jules Guerin to design and execute murals for the end walls and the ornamentation on the bronze ceiling beams. After more than 6 years of work at the site, the completed memorial was dedicated in a ceremony on Memorial Day, May 30, 1922. Chief Justice William Howard Taft, as chairman of the commission, presented the memorial to President Harding who accepted it for the United States.

ARCHITECTURE OF THE MEMORIAL

The memorial is of white Colorado-Yule marble. Its architectural lines are classical. The plan is similar to that of the Parthenon, the temple to the Goddess Athena on the Acropolis in Athens. The outer columns are Doric; the columns inside the great hall are Ionic. Together they represent Greek art at its perfection. The memorial building would not be out of place if set down among the great antiquities of Greece and Rome. Its beauty and purity of design equal the best of the ancient world.

Within the broad framework of classical design, the structure has a motif that symbolizes the Union of the States. Thirty-six columns, representing the 36 States in the Union at the time of Lincoln's death, surround the walls of the Memorial Building. A frieze above the colonnade names these States. On the attic walls above the frieze are the names of the 48 States comprising the Union at the time the memorial was built. Ernest C. Bairstow of Washington carved the frieze and the decorations of the attic wall.

Within the memorial chamber are three commemorative features, a colossal seated statue of Lincoln and two huge inscribed stone tablets. The marble statue of Lincoln occupies the place of honor. It is centrally located near the back of the chamber and faces the Washington Monument and the Capitol. A row of columns separates this central area from either end of the huge chamber. On the north wall inscribed in stone is Lincoln's Second Inaugural Address; on the south wall, similarly inscribed, is the Gettysburg Address.

The decorations of the Gettysburg and Second Inaugural Addresses were done under the direction of Daniel Chester French by Miss Evelyn Beatrice Longman, his assistant.

There are some structural features of the memorial not common in modern buildings. The columns are not vertical but are tilted slightly inward. The four corner columns have the greatest incline. The outer facade of the building above the columns also is tilted

Sculptor Daniel Chester French's colossal statue
of Lincoln in the central hall
reflects the gentle yet firm visage
of a war President.

inward, but less so than the columns. The walls of the building similarly incline inward, but less than either the colonnade and facade. This structural characteristic eliminates the optical illusion of bulging at the top.

The interior walls are Indiana limestone. The ceiling, 60 feet above the floor, includes bronze girders ornamented with laurel and oak leaves. The panels between the girders are Alabama marble saturated with paraffin to produce translucency. The floor and the wall base are pink Tennessee marble.

The 2 tripods, 1 on either side of the steps to the entrance of the memorial, are 9 feet high, each cut from a single block of pink Tennessee marble. The Piccirilli brothers of New York carved the tripods.

THE STATUE OF LINCOLN

Daniel Chester French designed and made the model for the statue of the seated Lincoln. It represents Lincoln as the War President.

Portrait of Lincoln taken shortly before his assassination in 1865.

The statue from head to foot is 19 feet high. The scale is such that if Lincoln were standing he would be 28 feet tall. The extreme width of the statue, including the drapery over the chair, is the same as its height—19 feet. There are 28 blocks of Georgia white marble in the sculptured statue. The Piccirilli brothers carved the stone in their New York studio, spending more than 4 years on the huge statue. Mr. French personally assisted in this work. Experiments with models showed that the statue, originally planned to be 10 feet tall, would be dwarfed and out of scale in the large hall where it would stand. This led to a change in the contract with Mr. French to double the size of the statue, so that it would be 19 or 20 feet tall.

FACTS AND FIGURES ABOUT THE BUILDING

Retaining Wall of Terrace Approach:
 Height, 14 feet.
 Length, 257 feet, east and west sides; width, 187 feet, 4 inches, north and south sides.

Foundation:
 44 to 65 feet to bedrock below original grade.

Height:
 80 feet above top of foundation.
 99 feet above grade at foot of terrace walls.

Colonnade:
 Length, 189 feet.
 Width, 118 feet, 8 inches.
 Number of columns, 36.
 Height of columns to cap, 44 feet.
 Diameter of column at base, 7 feet, 4 inches.
 Number of stone drums in column, 11.

Ionic Columns Inside Memorial:
 Height, 50 feet.
 Diameter at base, 5 feet, 6 inches.

Central Chamber with Seated Lincoln:
 Width, 58 feet.
 Depth, 74 feet.

Two End Chambers:
 Width, 63 feet.
 Depth, 36 feet, 8 inches.

Cost of Memorial Building, $2,957,000.

Cost of Lincoln Statue, $88,400.

55

14
Mesa Verde Cliff Dwellings

Cortez, Colo.

The Mesa Verde, Spanish for "green tables," rises high above the surrounding country. For about 1,300 years agricultural Indians occupied the mesa and surrounding regions and from the hundreds of ruins that remain archeologists have compiled one of the most significant chapters in the story of prehistoric America.

PREHISTORIC INHABITANTS OF THE MESA VERDE

The Mesa Verde was inhabited for about 1,300 years by agricultural Indians who began to drift into the area shortly after the beginning of the Christian Era. At first their culture was simple, but there was constant progress and by A.D. 1200 they had reached a high cultural level. Archeologists divide the long occupation into four archeological periods each of which has a descriptive name. They are not, of course, sharply marked; the dates given for each are approximate.

Basketmaker Period (A.D. 1 to 400). The first farming Indians of the Mesa Verde are called Basketmakers, because weaving of excellent baskets was their outstanding craft. At this early date three important things were unknown to the people: pottery, houses, and the bow and arrow. Since there was no pottery, baskets served for all household purposes for which containers were needed. The people lived in shallow caves that are common in this area, and perhaps, in summer, in brush huts near their fields on the mesa top. In the floors of the caves they built roofed pits (cists) for storage of corn and squash raised in small mesa-top fields. The atlatl, a primitive dart-throwing stick, was used for hunting and defense.

Once the farming culture was established,

Opposite
Square Tower Ruin, just one of several cliff dwelling sites at Mesa Verde.

the Basketmakers showed marked capacity for development and a willingness to borrow ideas from people with whom they came in contact. There was steady progress, and by the 400's significant changes took place.

Modified Basketmaker Period (A.D. 400 to 750). About the year 400 important new developments came. The Indians learned to make pottery and build roofed dwellings. Somewhat later, they began to use the bow and arrow. Although the people were still the same, the culture was changing. The early pottery was a plain, gray type that took the place of baskets for many uses such as cooking and water carrying. The dwellings were shallow pits with head-high roofs of poles and adobe. These provided ample protection from the weather, and the people were then able to live the year round on the open mesa tops in the midst of their corn fields.

The population seems to have increased rapidly, and soon there were hundreds of villages on the mesa tops and in caves of the Four Corners region. Toward the end of the period the architecture grew more elaborate. Rectangular rooms with vertical walls developed, and these were joined together to form large villages.

Developmental Pueblo Period (A.D. 750 to 1100). From about the year 750 on, the people showed an increasing tendency to group their houses together to form compact villages. To these a Spanish term, "pueblo," meaning village, has been given. It was a period of development and experimentation. Many types of house walls were tried: adobe, adobe and poles, stone slabs topped with adobe, adobe and stones, and finally true coursed masonry. The houses were joined together to form compact clusters around open courts and in these courts were pit houses that grew deeper and finally developed into ceremonial rooms, now called kivas.

As the result of much experimentation, pottery improved greatly during this period and certain definite types became associated with each area. Turkey-feather blankets became common, and the weaving of cotton cloth began. An odd development was a new carrying cradle which had a pronounced effect on the appearance of the people. During the Basketmaker periods a soft woven cradle had been used and the babies' heads developed normally. During the 800's the people adopted a cradle made of wood and as a result the heads of most of them were deformed, being noticeably flattened on the back.

The Developmental Pueblo Period was a time of peace, expansion, and progress. Innumerable farming villages dotted the region, the population increased, and arts and crafts showed constant improvement.

Great, or Classic, Pueblo Period (A.D. 1100 to 1300). As the name implies, this period marked the climax of the Pueblo culture in the Mesa Verde region, and arts and crafts reached the peak of their development. Houses were built of fine horizontal masonry of well-shaped stones laid in adobe mortar. Most of the walls were smoothly plastered, and designs painted in red, yellow, black, and white added a touch of color to the homes. Villages ranged in size from a few rooms and a single kiva to great terraced structures with as many as 200 rooms and more than a score of kivas.

The pottery was well-shaped, carefully fired, and elaborately decorated with geometrical and animal figures. The finely woven cotton cloth was often decorated with designs woven in color, and the jewelry was made of turquoise and other brightly colored stones.

A rigid social structure developed and a highly ritualistic religion evolved. The importance of this religion in the lives of the people is evidenced by the large number of ceremonial rooms and by the fact that separate buildings, designed solely for ceremonial use, were sometimes constructed.

For a time the culture flourished, establishing a peak of spectacular archeological significance. It was the classic period that produced such outstanding structures as Cliff Palace, Square Tower House, Spruce Tree House, Long House, Far View House.

Although the Pueblo culture reached its highest level during this period, there are evidences that adverse influences were affecting the people. During the 1100's most of the Pueblo Indians of the Mesa Verde lived on the open mesa tops in widely scattered villages, large and small. About A.D. 1200, there was a movement toward the caves and within a short time pueblos were built in most of the caves of the Mesa Verde.

There are numerous evidences that these cave pueblos, or cliff dwellings, were deliberately fortified, so it is apparent some danger faced the people. It is possible this resulted from a breakup within the tribe itself. There are many indications, however, that some new people, probably nomadic Indians, had moved into the area and had begun to harass the peaceful Pueblo farmers.

The end came quickly. Beginning in 1276, drought struck the region. For 24 years precipitation was deficient. Year after year the crops failed and the springs dried up. The only escape was to seek regions which had a more dependable water supply. Village after village was abandoned and before the drought ended all of the Indians had left the Mesa Verde, moving southward to New Mexico and Northern Arizona never to return.

THE RUINS

Ruins of many different types are accessible to Mesa Verde visitors. They range from pit houses built during the 500's to the cliff dwellings of the 1200's. The cliff dwellings are the most spectacular, but the mesa-top pit houses and pueblos are equally important for, seen in their chronological order, they show the architectural development of the Mesa Verde.

Pit Houses.—No ruins dating from early Basketmakers have been excavated in the Mesa Verde. During this earliest period, the people built storage cists and probably their first experimental houses in the caves. Later, the people built cliff dwellings in each cave so that now it will be necessary to excavate under the cliff dwellings to find evidence of the earliest people.

Two Modified Basketmaker pit houses may be seen by park visitors. The first was built shortly before A.D. 600. Although it once had a roof as high as a man's head, nothing remains but the underground part of the house. The pit, roughly circular, is 20 feet in diameter and 30 inches deep, with a fire-pit in the center. Four holes in the floor indicate the position of the four posts which once supported the roof of poles, bark, and adobe. South of this main room is a smaller antechamber. This was also roofed over and was connected with the larger room by a covered passageway. The entrance probably was a small door in the south wall of the antechamber. The smoke hole in the roof of the main room served as an additional entrance.

The second pit house, built a century later, shows certain very definite changes. The antechamber has disappeared and in its place is a vertical shaft that served as a ventilator and entrance. This D-shaped pit house is much deeper than the earlier structure, and a wide bench is present on three sides of the room. This structure shows definite similarities to the kivas into which the pit houses developed at a later date.

The earliest pit houses were sometimes built in the caves, but after A. D. 600, most of the people built their houses out in the open.

Pueblo Ruins.—The wider canyon bottoms and the mesa tops are dotted with scores,

Sun Temple, on the canyon's rim, apparently was a religious sanctuary.

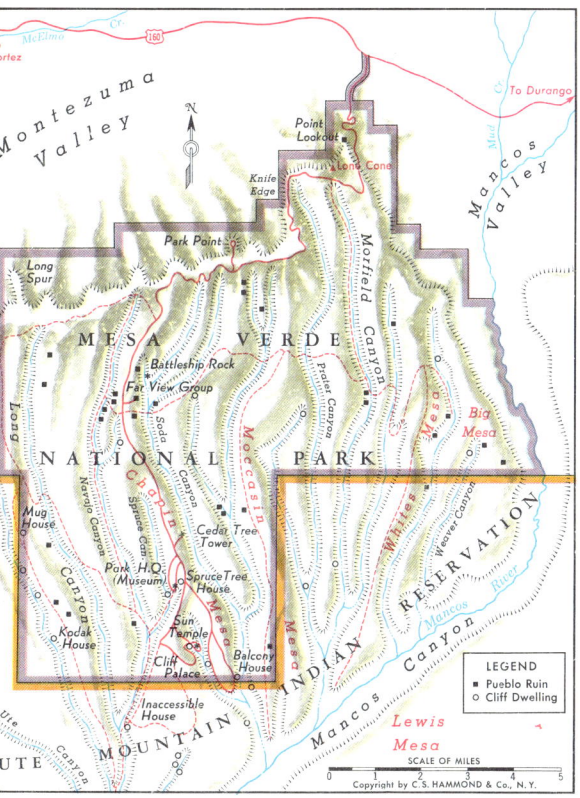

perhaps hundreds, of pueblo ruins dating from both the Developmental and Great Pueblo Periods.

The first pueblos, built during the 800's, were constructed of thin stone slabs, poles, and adobe. The small, rectangular, flat-roofed houses were joined together in long rows, and in the court south of the houses were one or more deep pit rooms. Later, stone masonry came into use, and the pit rooms developed into kivas.

After stone masonry came into general use, it improved rapidly. During the 1100's, the thick walls of the mesa-top pueblos were made of well-cut blocks of stone laid in adobe mortar. At this time an important change was made in the plan of the pueblos. Formerly, the kivas, which were used chiefly by the men, were located outside the house structure, being some distance to the south. During the 1100's, the kivas were built in the midst of the village and were surrounded by the house walls. Often high towers were constructed in the pueblos. Placing the kivas inside the walls, and building high towers, which probably served as watchtowers, perhaps indicate that the Pueblo Indians were faced with some new danger.

Cliff Dwellings.—During the last century of the Great Pueblo Period (A.D. 1200-1300), most of the Pueblo Indians of the Mesa Verde left the mesa tops and built their homes in the caves that abound in the many canyons. It is possible this was done for security from harassment by some other tribe of Indians.

Cliff Palace, the largest and most famous, was the first major cliff dwelling discovered in the Mesa Verde. This large village, built under the protecting roof of a tremendous cave on the east wall of Cliff Canyon, contains over 200 living rooms and may have sheltered as many as 400 people. Cliff Palace is notable for its vast size and for the amazing amount of masonry it contains.

59

15
Minute Man Statue

Concord, Mass.

There was crisis in the air, sharper than any man on the green realized. A few Boston Whigs had hoped to lure the British regulars out into the countryside, where they could be dealt with more easily. And when he had heard of the first shots, Samuel Adams cried, "O! What a glorious morning is this."

For six generations throughout New England, the common people had governed themselves. Each town even chose its own minister, and each church determined its own form of faith. They had always defined their liberties as "the rights of Englishmen," and now as loyal Englishmen they were determined to defend themselves against Parliament.

The British imperial system was, in fact, the most liberal the world had ever seen and inflicted no oppression. But the Empire had recently endured a world war (the Seven Years War, touched off by young George Washington at Fort Necessity on the frontier), and victory had brought new territory, new responsibilities, and greater expenses. The British Ministry believed not only that the American colonies should contribute toward the cost of maintaining the western garrisons and the British fleet which protected their shipping but also that Parliament possessed the power to tax the colonists. When Lord Grenville, the King's chief minister, invited the colonists to share these costs, they protested that the proposed taxes would be unconstitutional and a dangerous precedent. To maintain order and prop up the Massachusetts Bay government, regulars were then sent to Boston.

Resolving to nip revolution in the bud, the Ministry in London authorized Gen. Thomas Gage to take action. Gage knew that military stores were being gathered in Concord to oppose his authority as Governor of Massachusetts. So on the night of April 18, 1775, he sent some 700 regulars (the light infantry and grenadier companies of several regiments) in boats across the Charles River to begin their march on the rebels' stores. Their commanders were Lt. Col. Francis Smith, whose incompetence would be responsible for the the outbreak of war, and Maj. John Pitcairn of the Royal Marines, an able soldier and a charming gentleman who was popular among the Americans.

After having lanterns hung in a church steeple to alert the waiting Whigs, Paul Revere crossed the river to Charlestown and rode out to alarm the countryside. About midnight Revere reached Lexington and warned Samuel Adams and John Hancock. Joined by William Dawes, another messenger who had taken a longer route from Boston, and Dr. Samuel Prescott of Concord, Revere continued his ride. A British patrol intercepted the party in Lincoln and took Revere into brief custody. Dawes was forced to turn back, but Prescott eluded capture and carried the warning on to Concord.

Moving with fatal slowness, Smith did not arrive in Lexington until daylight of the 19th. As the redcoats marched up, William Diamond beat out a drum call for the militia to reassemble. When Pitcairn and his officers reached the green, they saw to their great relief that there were only about half of the Lexington company drawn up in two ranks. The head of the militia, John Parker, who never intended to block the vastly superior British force, ordered his men to disperse and not fire. Pitcairn also called upon his men not to fire (the light infantry was now chasing the Americans) but to surround the militia. Then tragedy struck, as the provincials moved toward the crowd. A shot rang out. Other shots followed. Then, acting without orders, two platoons of the first light infantry company poured a volley into the backs of the retiring militiamen. Pitcairn ordered a ceasefire, but the soldiers, their own colonels absent, ignored the major and kept up an irregular fire. After furiously berating their men for disobeying orders, the British officers reformed the column and picked up the march to Concord, leaving behind 8 American dead and 10 wounded.

After news of the skirmish reached Concord, 7 miles away, three companies from that town and two from Lincoln set off down the Lexington road until they saw the British column about a mile away. The provincials waited as the regulars closed. Then they faced about and by marching along the ridge which parallels the road escorted the regulars into town, their fifes and drums joining those of the British in "grand musick." It was about 8 a.m. when Smith and his forces reached Concord. While one company of light infantry held the South Bridge, seven others were sent to secure the North Bridge and to destroy the military stores at Col. James Barrett's farm, which lay 2 miles beyond. In the face of this force, the militia pulled back across the North Bridge to higher ground on Punkatasset Hill, 1 mile away, where they were joined by fresh companies from neighboring towns.

In the Concord townhouse the regulars found a large store of gun carriages, which they piled nearby and set on fire. The building also caught, and the officers might have let it burn if the townspeople had not persuaded them to put out the fire.

To the north, the Americans, now reinforced, left Punkatasset Hill, marched toward the British stationed on the hill west of the North Bridge, and forced them to retreat to a position on the road at the west end of the bridge. While the provincials deliberated on their next move, the three infantry companies also waited but without planning how they would defend the bridge. When the Americans saw the smoke from the burning stores, they thought that the town was on fire and set out to investigate. The British fell back across the bridge to the Concord side, taking up a few planks on the way. As the provincials came on, the regulars fired shots into the water, then into the advancing ranks. The Americans returned the fire from along the banks and made untenable the position of the redcoats, who fled toward Concord. Pursuing them only to the first turn, the minute men and militia took up positions on the ridge overlooking the road, which Smith came marching along with reinforcements.

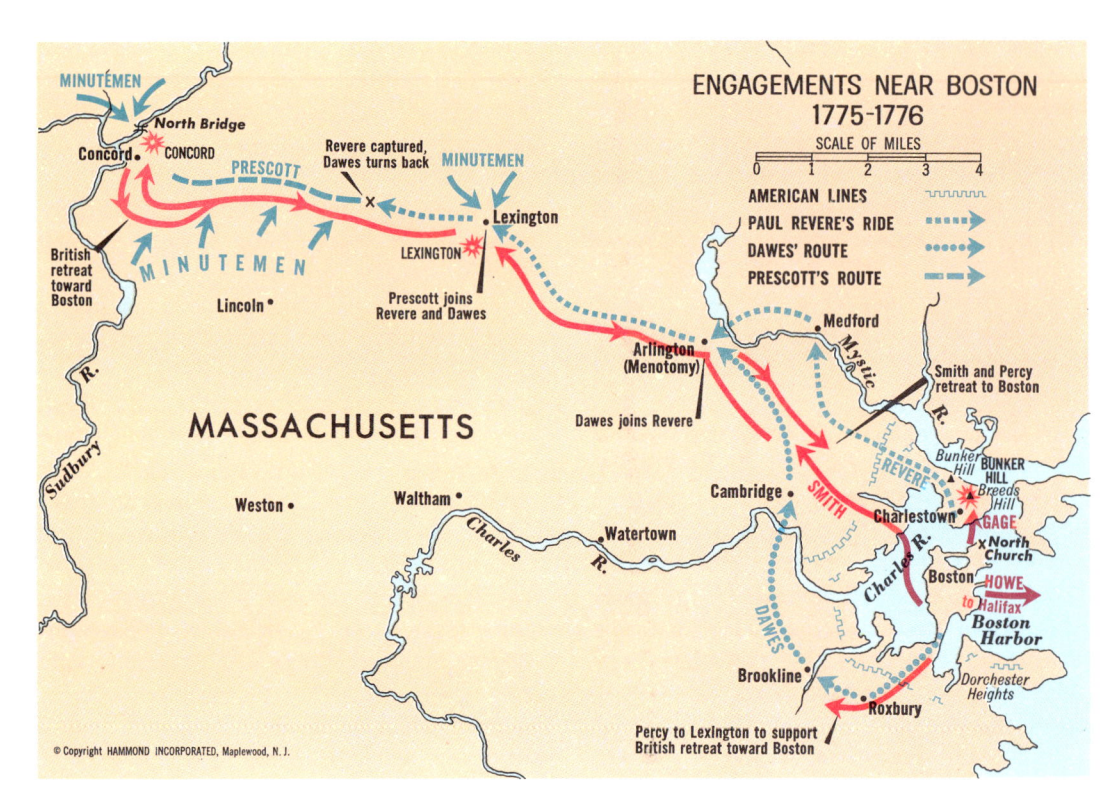

The colonists who had chased the infantry from the bridge now returned to the high ground on the west side of the river. Had they taken up the bridge, they could probably have cornered the detachment coming back from Barrett's farm. But the Americans only watched the regulars march by. Upon crossing the bridge, the British were horrified to find that a Concord youth had taken a hatchet to one of their wounded, and they carried to the troops in the village the story that the Americans were scalping their fallen.

With his forces reunited and the captured stores destroyed, Colonel Smith prepared to return to Boston. The scarlet column set out about noon on the long eastward march. At Meriam's Corner, the column reformed on the road to cross a bridge. As the flankers slowly descended the ridge, a minute company from Reading arrived just ahead of other companies from the towns to the north and took cover on the Meriam farm. Across the Lexington road some of the men who had chased the redcoats away from the North Bridge waited for another crack at them. Here, for the third time that day, shots were exchanged.

In steadily increasing numbers the Colonialists took cover along the march route to shoot at the retreating redcoats, who saw now that they would have to fight all the way back to Boston. In Lincoln, about 1 mile beyond Meriam's Corner, the British had to pass through a gauntlet of fire delivered by Americans. As the British continued toward Lexington, the fire slackened but never entirely ceased. A shot hit Pitcairn's horse. Smith was wounded in the leg. Nearly out of powder and ball and with the flankers too exhausted to be effective, the regulars approached Lexington Green in a state of near panic. All knew that to survive they had to receive reinforcements. These they now saw — fresh scarlet ranks drawn up near where they had loaded their guns at daylight. It was 2:30 p.m.

Hugh, Earl Percy left Boston that morning with 1,000 men and 2 fieldpieces. Taking the long route, he passed through Roxbury and Cambridge, where he found the bridge over the Charles dismantled. The thrifty Yankees had neatly piled up the planks nearby, so the soldiers crossed over on the stringers and quickly repaired the bridge. Moving with swift efficiency, Percy pressed on to a point on the Lexington road where he could place his cannon effectively and establish a position that would give Smith's shattered army a rest.

The British well knew that they were still in great danger. While the rebels' numbers were likely to increase, there was little hope that Gage could either reinforce or resupply them; and the road back to Boston could be obstructed in many places, disrupting the march and making easier targets of the bewildered British. By the prevailing code, the Americans had conducted themselves like barbarians. Civilians firing upon any French or German army risked the murder of every man, woman, and child and the burning of every building in sight. Percy did burn three houses in Lexington from which sniping could be expected. But as his force marched back toward Boston, his officers did their best to prevent the destruction of private property.

The most severe fighting of the day occurred as the combined British forces moved out from Lexington. At Menotomy (present Arlington), and Cambridge, many of the Americans who fired at the British from the cover of houses were caught from behind and bayoneted. (Nearly half of the Americans killed that day died in Menotomy.) At what is now Porter Square in Cambridge, the Americans tried to divert the regulars toward the partly dismantled bridge over the Charles. The British forced their way through and continued on toward Charlestown. Arriving after dark, they embarked for Boston, thoroughly shaken by their experience and its implications. They had suffered 273 casualties to 93 for the Americans, and they were certain that the next time one of their armies was caught in such a situation, not a man would escape.

Immediately after the battle, affidavits were taken from scores of participants and witnesses. The Whig politicians broadcast a version of events that would have made Attila blush. Fired by such stories the English Whigs openly and vigorously opposed the war, in Parliament as well as in the Army and Navy, and made firm execution of it almost impossible.

When the news of Lexington and Concord reached the middle and Southern colonies, civil wars of a different pattern broke out—to merge into a single struggle and eventually end in independence for the Thirteen Colonies. Today, many observers trace the beginning of the end of the world's colonial systems back to April 19, 1775. The shots fired then still reverberate around the world.

The Minute Man Statue by Daniel Chester French occupies the site of the American position at the historic North Bridge battle at Concord. It was erected there on the centennial in 1875.

16
Mount Rushmore

Keystone, S. Dak.

The faces of the four American Presidents carved into 6,000-foot Mount Rushmore boldly symbolize the vigorous beginnings and trials of the United States during its first century and a half of growth. Washington represents the struggle for independence and the birth of the Republic. Jefferson expresses the country's political philosophy of self-government—a government of the people, by the people, and for the people. Lincoln typifies the permanency of the Nation and the struggle to assure equality for all its citizens. And Theodore Roosevelt depicts 20th-century America, a period which awakened the people to the necessity for conserving the natural resources and saw the United States emerge as a determining influence in world affairs.

The idea of a gigantic sculpture in the Black Hills originated in 1923 with Doane Robinson, State historian of South Dakota. In the beginning, he considered carving, on the granite formation known as the Needles, the figures of romantic western heroes such as Jim Bridger, John Colter, and Kit Carson. The proposal met with only moderate public acceptance, but authorization for funds to carry the work forward were obtained.

At the invitation of Robinson, Gutzon Borglum came to the Black Hills to study the proposal in the autumn of 1924. Borglum, a sculptor then at work on a Confederate memorial on Stone Mountain in Georgia, immediately saw an opportunity to create a memorial of national significance and suggested Presidents as subjects. A location other than the Needles was needed, and after much searching Borglum selected Mount Rushmore, because it was of smooth-grained granite, dominated the surrounding terrain, and faced the sun most of the day.

Work on the mountain began on August 10, 1927, the same day President Calvin Coolidge officially dedicated Mount Rushmore as a National Memorial. Lack of funds

Below
The Lincoln carving as it appeared in 1940 showing the scaffolding & methods of work.

and bad weather delayed the project frequently, and 14 years were required to bring the sculpture to its present appearance.

In the early years, private donations supported the project, but when more funds were required, the Federal Government assumed full financial responsibility. Federal appropriations accounted for $836,000 of the $989,992 spent on the memorial.

In March 1941, before he could finish the memorial, Gutzon Borglum died. His son, Lincoln, continued to work on it until funds were exhausted later the same year. Since then, no additional carving has been done on the mountain and there are no plans to add other figures to the group.

MOUNTAIN "CARVING"

The word "carving" used in connection with Mount Rushmore is only a figure of speech, since very few conventional sculpturing methods were employed. "A unique engineering accomplishment" better describes the work performed in creating the memorial.

Gutzon Borglum used engineering techniques at Mount Rushmore that he had developed earlier during his work on Stone Mountain. His first task was to design a Presidential grouping that would conform to the mountain's granite cap. Deep cracks and fissures required nine changes in his basic design. Next he made individual working models of each President to guide the workmen on the mountain. The models measured 5 feet from chin to the top of the head.

Measurements of the models were made with a plumb bob from a horizontal bar and transferred to the mountain through a 30-foot movable boom. One inch on a model equaled 12 inches on the mountain. Once a reference point was located, such as the tip of the nose, excess rock could be removed with dynamite. More than 450,000 tons of rock were removed by this method.

Drillers, suspended over the face of the mountain in "swing seats" controlled by hand-operated winches, used jackhammers to drill holes for the dynamite. Blasting removed excess rock to within 3 to 4 inches of the final surface. Holes were then drilled vertically over the surface at intervals of about 3 inches. The remaining rock was wedged off with a small drill and, in some cases, with a hammer and a wedging tool. The sculpture was brought to a smooth finish with a small air hammer, by a process known as "bumping."

The faces were carved to a scale of men 465 feet tall. On an average, the heads measure 60 feet from chin to top, with each nose 20 feet long, each mouth 18 feet wide, and the eyes 11 feet across. Borglum did not intend for Mount Rushmore to become known only for its gigantic proportions; rather, he believed that "a monument's dimensions should be determined by the importance to civilization of the events commemorated."

65

17
Saratoga Battlefield

Stillwater, N.Y.

"Rebellion which a twelve-month ago was a contemptible pygmy, is now in appearance a giant." So spoke a contemporary after the Battle of Saratoga. Burgoyne's surrender on October 17, 1777, was one of those signal events that shape the destiny of nations. The American success encouraged a hesitant France to intervene openly on the side of the colonists. Without this support, America's bid for liberty might have been lost. At home, Saratoga was equally decisive. Though 4 more years of fighting were necessary to bring final victory at Yorktown, the battle furnished the physical and psychological impetus that brightened a desperate cause at a moment when failure would have been disastrous.

THE BURGOYNE CAMPAIGN

For centuries the Lake Champlain-Hudson River route had been a strategic highway through the northeast. In pre-Revolutionary years this route was bloodied during the wars between England and France for control of North America. Once again it was to be a theater of historic events, this time unfolding the drama of a people aiming to establish a free nation.

Burgoyne's plan for the campaign of 1777 called for his army to move southward from Canada along the Champlain-Hudson route; Col. Barry St. Leger was to march east from Lake Ontario along the Mohawk River; and simultaneously Sir William Howe was to move up the Hudson from New York City. The three forces were to unite at Albany under Howe's command. Thus the British armies of Canada and New York would be combined. The British leaders hoped that this strong force could quickly end the rebellion.

The crux of Burgoyne's thinking was the three-pronged movement on Albany. But unknown to him until late in the campaign, Colonial Secretary George Germain had approved an additional plan proposed by General Howe. Instead of heading for Albany, Howe undertook a seaborne expedition against Philadelphia, the patriot Capital. He left only a small force under Sir Henry Clinton to act on the Hudson.

Germain had endorsed Howe's plan trusting that he would return to New York in time to cooperate with Burgoyne. But Howe was already at sea and deeply committed to the Philadelphia campaign when he received Germain's conditional approval. Thus, except for an ineffective sally up the Hudson by Clinton, Burgoyne would have to fend for himself.

To succeed, Burgoyne's campaign depended on mutually supporting armies. When his army advanced from Canada without support from New York City, it became an isolated column in a vast and hostile wilderness.

Burgoyne embarked from St. Johns (now St. Jean), Canada, on June 17, 1777. His total force of 9,400 men included some 4,200 British regulars, 4,000 German troops, and several hundred Canadians and Indians. Confidently, Burgoyne advanced southward to attack Ticonderoga on Lake Champlain. On July 6, after a 4-day siege, the fort fell.

Moving on southward through Skenesboro, Fort Ann, and Fort Edward, Burgoyne was impeded by rough terrain and the delaying tactics of Gen. Philip Schuyler, then commanding American forces in the Northern Department. Schuyler's troops felled trees, destroyed bridges, and burned crops before the path of the British.

Time and the tide of events now began to run against the British. St. Leger halted his advance down the Mohawk Valley to besiege Fort Stanwix. In the battle of Oriskany, August 6, he stopped an American column marching to aid the fort. But learning that a strong relief force was on its way, he raised the siege and retreated toward Canada.

Even more serious was the fate of the detachment Burgoyne sent to Bennington, Vt. On August 16 John Stark's and Seth Warner's New England militia shattered this force, inflicting about 800 casualties.

Despite these setbacks, Burgoyne decided to sever his communications with Canada and risk all on a push to Albany. On September 13 he crossed to the west bank of the Hudson at Saratoga (now Schuylerville) and began marching southward toward Albany.

Four miles north of the village of Stillwater, Burgoyne came upon the Americans, 9,000 strong. In command now was Gen. Horatio Gates, who had replaced Schuyler. The Americans were entrenched on Bemis Heights, a strong position where the road to Albany squeezed through a defile between the hills and river, as does today's U.S. 4.

American artillery on the heights and in redoubts along the Hudson commanded the road and the river. Burgoyne's heavily burdened army had to pass through this defile to get to Albany, for the surrounding country was rough and roadless. Thaddeus Kosciuszko, a Polish military engineer serving with the Americans, had chosen and fortified the site. Burgoyne chose to attack.

THE BATTLE OPENS AT FREEMAN FARM

On September 19 the Royal Army advanced upon the American camp in three separate columns. Two of them headed through the heavy forests covering the region; the other, composed of German troops, marched down the river road.

American scouts operating on the east side of the Hudson detected Burgoyne's army in motion. When advised of this, Gates ordered Col. Daniel Morgan's corps to reconnoiter the enemy's march. About 12:30 p.m. a detachment of Morgan's men brushed with the advance guard of Burgoyne's center column in a clearing known as the Freeman Farm.

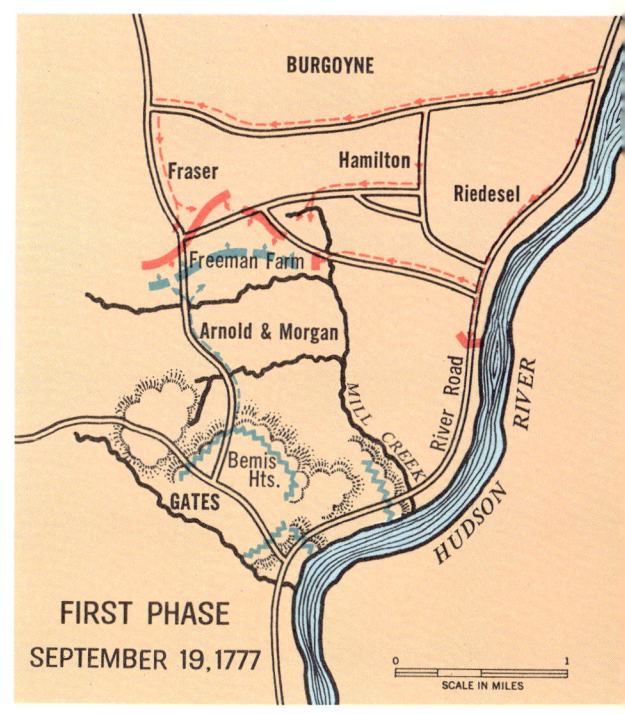

Unique monument to Arnold's wounded leg.

Action was renewed after a brief lull, and for more than 3 hours fighting swayed back and forth over the farm. Repeatedly the British regiments had to re-form their lines and charge with fixed bayonets, only to be stopped short by the deadly fire of American riflemen, who used natural cover to great advantage. It was European tactics against frontier tactics; and in this forested, ravine-slashed terrain irregular riflemen won out.

Under the skillful direction of Gen. Benedict Arnold, American reinforcements were placed where they threatened to outflank the British right. At this crucial point, German reinforcements arrived from the river road. Hurling them against the American right, Burgoyne steadied the wavering British line and gradually forced the Americans to withdraw. Except for this arrival and near exhaustion of the American's ammunition, Burgoyne might have been defeated that day.

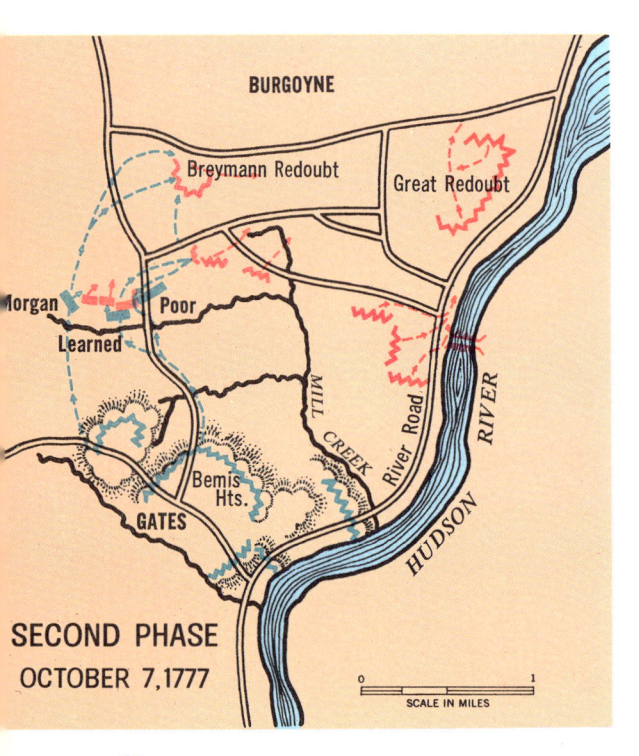

Though he possessed the immediate field of battle, Burgoyne's advance had been stopped about 1 mile north of the American line and his army roughly treated. Shaken by this "victory," Burgoyne ordered his troops to entrench in the vicinity of the Freeman Farm and awaited help from Clinton who was preparing to move toward Albany from New York City.

Nearly 3 weeks of anxious waiting brought no aid from the south. True, Clinton did capture the forts along the Hudson on October 6; but Burgoyne did not know this; nor was Clinton's distant success an immediate threat to Gates.

THE DRIVE ON BEMIS HEIGHTS

By now Burgoyne's situation was critical. Faced by a growing American army (4,000 militiamen had heeded Gates' call), without hope of help from the south, and supplies rapidly diminishing, the British army became weaker each passing day. Burgoyne had to choose between advancing or retreating. He decided to risk a second engagement.

On October 7 Burgoyne ordered a reconnaissance-in-force to test the American left flank. Ably led, and supported by 10 cannon, a force of 1,500 men moved out of the British camp.

After marching southwesterly about three-quarters of a mile, the troops deployed in a clearing on the Barber farm. The larger part of the British front faced an open field, but both flanks rested in woods, thus exposing them to surprise attack by the enemy.

As the Royal Army advanced, the American scouts retired and the alarm was beaten in Gates' camp. About 3 p.m. the Americans attacked in three columns under Colonel Morgan, Gen. Ebenezer Learned, and Gen. Enoch Poor. Repeatedly the British line was broken, then rallied; both flanks were severely punished and driven back.

The Schuyler House erected in 1777 shortly after Burgoyne's surrender replaced an earlier house burned by the British.

At this critical point, Gen. Simon Fraser, who commanded the right wing of the British column, rode among his men in a desperate effort to encourage a stand and cover the developing withdrawal. In the fog of battle, Fraser was mortally wounded and had to be borne from the field.

Before the enemy's flanks could be rallied, Arnold—without command, following a quarrel with Gates—rode onto the field and led Learned's brigade against the German troops holding the British center. Under tremendous pressure from all sides, the Germans joined a general withdrawal into the fortifications on the Freeman Farm.

Within an hour after the opening clash, Burgoyne lost 8 cannon and over 400 officers and men. Flushed with success, the Americans believed victory was near. Led by Arnold, one column launched a series of savage attacks on the Balcarres Redoubt, a powerful position on the Freeman Farm.

After repeated attacks failed to carry this position, Arnold wheeled his horse and, dashing through the crossfire of both armies, spurred northwest to the Breymann Redoubt. He arrived as American troops began to assault the front and left of the fortification. Arnold joined them in the final surge that overwhelmed the redoubt. Upon entering the work, he was wounded in the leg. Had he died there, posterity would have known few names brighter than that of Benedict Arnold.

Darkness ended the day's fighting, saving Burgoyne from immediate disaster.

RETREAT AND SURRENDER

That night Burgoyne withdrew his troops behind the Great Redoubt, which protected the high ground and river flats at the northeast corner of the battlefield. The next night, after burying General Fraser in the redoubt, the British began their retreat northward. Burgoyne had suffered 1,000 casualties in the fighting of the past 3 weeks; American losses numbered less than 500.

After a miserable march in mud and rain, Burgoyne's troops took refuge in a fortified camp on the heights at Saratoga. There an American force that had grown to nearly 20,000 men surrounded his exhausted army. In the face of these great odds Burgoyne was forced to surrender on October 17, 1777. By the terms of the Convention of Saratoga, Burgoyne's depleted army, some 6,000 men, marched out of their camp "with the Honors of War," and stacked their arms along the west bank of the Hudson.

THE SCHUYLER HOUSE

Situated in Schuylerville (historic Saratoga), this estate was the country home of Gen. Philip Schuyler both before and after the battle. When the British retreated to Saratoga, they burned the buildings of General Schuyler's estate. The British and American commissioners who drew up surrender terms met on the Schuyler property.

69

18
Statue of Liberty

New York, N.Y.

The Statue of Liberty was conceived and designed as a symbol of a great international friendship. With the passing of the years its significance has deepened until today it is the most symbolic structure in the United States.

Standing in New York Harbor at the very portal of the New World, the Statue of Liberty, one of the most colossal sculptures in the history of the world, has greeted many millions of the oppressed and of the venturesome of other lands who have crossed the ocean in hopeful search of greater freedom and opportunity. To them, and to the whole world, the statue has become the symbol of those ideals of human liberty upon which our Nation and its form of government were founded.

To the poet Emma Lazarus, who saw refugees from persecution arriving on a tramp steamer, following incredible sufferings, the statue was "The New Colossus." She wrote of it in 1883:

Not like the brazen giant of Greek fame,
With conquering limbs astride from land to land;
Here at our sea-washed, sunset gates shall stand
A mighty woman with a torch, whose flame
Is the imprisoned lightning, and her name
Mother of Exiles. From her beacon-hand
Glows world-wide welcome; her mild eyes command
The air-bridged harbor that twin cities frame.
"Keep ancient lands, your storied pomp!" cries she
With silent lips. "Give me your tired, your poor,
Your huddled masses yearning to breathe free,
The wretched refuse of your teeming shore.
Send these, the homeless, tempest-tost to me,
I lift my lamp beside the golden door!"

In its international aspect the statue, which was a gift from the people of France to the people of the United States, commemorates the long friendship between the peoples of the two Nations—a friendship that has continued since the American Revolution when France helped turn the tide of victory to the side of the Colonies.

PLAN APPROVED AND FUND RAISING UNDERTAKEN

In 1865 French historian Edouard de Laboulaye proposed that a memorial be built to mark the alliance of France and the United States during the American Revolution. It was to be a joint undertaking by both countries, and an Alsatian sculptor, Frederick Auguste Bartholdi, was sent to America to study and discuss the project.

After his arrival in the United States, Bartholdi conceived of a colossal statue standing in New York Harbor, at the gateway to the New World, representing not only the friendship of two nations but a common heritage—liberty.

Bartholdi's conception of the international memorial was accepted, and in November 1875 the Franco-American Union was formed to make plans, secure funds, and prosecute the program.

Edouard de Laboulaye was named president of the Union, and among its members were the most notable names in France. It was decided that the finished work of the entire monument would represent the joint effort of the two nations. The French people would build the statue and transport it to the United States; and the American people would build the pedestal on which it was to stand.

The response of the people of France was quick and warm, and a campaign to raise the necessary funds was launched with public entertainments. The cost of the statue was greater than anticipated, but by the end of 1879 the required amount—$250,000—had been collected. All of it was contributed by popular subscription, and governmental assistance was not required.

CONSTRUCTION OF THE STATUE

As soon as Bartholdi's plan had been approved by the men who sent him to America, he had started working on the designs.

Enlarged sectional model of left hand of the statue during construction.

The most difficult problems were involved in the mechanics of construction. In solving them the sculptor had no guide but his own genius. The material for it must be light, easily worked, of good appearance and yet strong enough to stand the stress of a long ocean voyage—and must be almost impervious to the effect of the salt-laden air of New York Harbor. Copper was decided upon as the material, to be supported by a framework of iron and steel.

To get the form for the statue, Bartholdi made what is called the study model, measuring about 4 feet in height. This was cast and recast. From this model was reproduced a statue having a height of 9 feet. By this method another model four times larger was obtained, giving the figure a height of 36 feet. This model was corrected down to the most minute detail. Then the statue was divided into a large number of sections, each of which was also to be reproduced four times its size. These reproductions, when joined together, were destined for the colossal statue in its finished form.

Only a comparatively small portion of such a gigantic statue could be worked on at a time. Section by section, the 36-foot model was enlarged to four times its size. For each section of the enlarged model it was necessary to take about 9,000 separate measurements. When a section was finished, the carpenters made wooden molds.

On these molds, copper sheets, 3/32-inch thick, were pressed and hammered into shape. More than 300 separate sheets of copper, each hand-hammered over an individual mold, went into the outside, or envelope, of the statue to form the figure.

The framework, too, is worthy of attention. It was designed and executed by the great French engineer, Gustave Eiffel, who afterwards constructed the famous Eiffel Tower in Paris. Four huge iron posts run from the base of the statue to the top, forming a pylon which bears the weight of the whole structure. Out of this central tower is built a maze of smaller beams, each supporting a series of outer copper sheets. Each sheet is backed by an iron strap to give it rigidity. These iron straps are fastened to the supporting framework in such a way that each section is supported independently—no plate of copper hangs from the one above it or bears upon the one below.

The present green coating of the statue, a patina, is the result of oxidation of copper. The construction is remarkable when one considers that the width of the face is 10 feet and that of the eyes 2 feet and 6 inches; and that the arm carrying the torch is 42 feet long and 12 feet in diameter at the point of greatest thickness.

The arm of the statue which carries the torch was exhibited in Philadelphia in 1876 at the Centennial Celebration of American Independence. Later in the same year it was exhibited at Madison Square in New York City and then returned to France. The head of the statue was shown in Paris at a World's Fair held there in 1878.

In the completed statue the shackle, which Liberty symbolically has broken, lies in front of her right foot, the heel of which is raised as in walking. The shackle chain disappears beneath the draperies and reappears in front of her left foot, the end link modeled to appear broken.

AMERICANS BUILD THE PEDESTAL

Meanwhile an American committee started to raise funds for the construction of the pedestal on Bedloe's Island (now Liberty Island) in New York Harbor. It was decided that the pedestal should be built in the center of old Fort Wood, an 11-pointed star-shaped fort constructed early in the nineteenth century to protect New York.

The American efforts to raise funds for building the pedestal were hampered by public apathy. The estimated cost of $150,000 fell far short of the actual funds required. Work on the pedestal stopped completely in the autumn of 1884 with only 15 feet of the structure completed and all funds exhausted. An additional $100,000 was needed before construction could continue, but the public was reluctant to contribute further.

In March 1885, the *New York World,* which had earlier undertaken to popularize the pedestal campaign, renewed its crusade for contributions. In daily editorials Joseph Pulitzer, publisher of the *World* and himself an immigrant, assailed public indifference and urged benefit performances, sporting events, and entertainments for the necessary funds. Pulitzer's efforts were so successful that, in less than 5 months, the money was raised.

With the solving of the financial problem in 1885, work was resumed, the builders then turning their attention to a highly important engineering problem—how the statue would resist wind pressure.

When the 29-foot level was reached in construction of the pedestal, four huge girders were built into the walls so that they formed a square across the inside. Fifty-five feet higher—a few feet from the top of the pedestal — similar girders were placed, and the two sets were connected by the iron tie beams which continued on up and became part of the framework of the statue itself. Thus the statue was made an integral part of the pedestal, and any force exerted upon it was carried down to the 29-foot level, so that the great weight of the upper 60 feet of the granite and concrete pedestal was added to that of the statue. The pedestal itself is considered one of the heaviest pieces of masonry ever built. It towers 89 feet above its foundation and is so anchored to it—and that in turn to the rock below the foundation—that a windstorm, to overturn the statue, would almost have to invert the whole island. General Charles P. Stone, engineer in charge of the construction, evolved the method of an-

Statue of Liberty in a patriotic needlepoint design. This earlier version was done by an Arab immigrant.

chorage and his careful calculations have been proved by the test of years.

On April 22, 1886, the last stone of the pedestal was swung into place and the jubilant workmen showered into the mortar a collection of silver coins from their own pockets.

Now the stage was set to receive and place in position the generous gift from the people of France.

COMPLETION AND DEDICATION
OF THE STATUE

During all the furor of fund raising and pedestal building in the United States, Bartholdi in France had continued to work on his colossal statue. In a letter to the chairman of the American Committee, dated December 19, 1882, he wrote: "Our work advances. The Statue commences to reach above the houses, and by next spring we shall see it over-look the entire city, as the large monuments of Paris now do."

By 1884, all the pieces of the statue had been put together and it stood a veritable colossus overlooking all the roof tops of Paris. Bartholdi had given 10 years of his life to the great work, putting into it both his ability as a sculptor and his love of freedom. July 4 was the day selected for the formal delivery of the statue. On that day Count Ferdinand de Lesseps, builder of the Suez Canal, who had succeeded De Laboulaye as president of the Franco-American Union, presented to the United States, the colossal Statue of Liberty.

By January 1885, the work of shipping the statue to America was completed. Each piece was classified and marked so that it could be reassembled on Bedloe's Island with accuracy and efficiency. The pieces were packed in 214 specially constructed cases which, when filled, varied in weight from a few hundred pounds to several tons.

The French Government supplied a vessel, the *Isere,* in which to transport the statue to the United States. The *Isere* left Rouen on May 21, 1885, and arrived at Sandy Hook, at the entrance of New York Harbor, on June 17. After the title papers to the statue had been transferred to General Stone, the vessel was docked at Bedloe's Island.

The Statue of Liberty Enlightening the World was dedicated October 28, 1886. Count de Lesseps was among the speakers. Bartholdi, in the torch some 300 feet above, pulled the rope that removed the French tricolor from Liberty's face. Then, President Grover Cleveland accepted the statue on behalf of the United States. Especially impressive were these words of his: "We will not forget that Liberty has here made her home; nor shall her chosen altar be neglected."

That night the torch held high in the hand of the statue was lighted.

DIMENSIONS OF THE STATUE

	Ft.	In.
Height from base to torch	151	1
Foundation of pedestal to torch	305	1
Heel to top of head	111	1
Length of hand	16	5
Index finger	8	0
Circumference at second joint	3	6
Size of fingernail, 13 x 10 inches		
Head from chin to cranium	17	3
Head thickness from ear to ear	10	0
Distance across the eye	2	6
Length of nose	4	6
Right arm, length	42	0
Right arm, greatest thickness	12	0
Thickness of waist	35	0
Width of mouth	3	0
Tablet, length	23	7
Tablet, width	13	7
Tablet, thickness	2	0
Height of granite pedestal	89	0
Height of foundation	65	0

Weight of copper used in statue, 200,000 pounds
Weight of steel used in statue, 250,000 pounds
Total weight of statue, 450,000 pounds (225 tons)
Copper sheeting of statue is 3/32-inch thick

Lighting this gigantic structure to best advantage was a perplexing problem. The system of electric lights originally installed has been replaced several times by more modern equipment. Today, the statue is floodlighted at night by ninety-six 1,000-watt lamps located at the base, with incidental lights introduced at certain points on the statue to eliminate undesirable shadows. The torch itself is lighted by thirteen 1,000-watt lamps.

Through the years this bright symbol of liberty and freedom has been under the care of the Lighthouse Board, the War Department, and the National Park Service. In 1924 the Statue of Liberty was declared a National Monument, and in 1965 Congress changed the island's name to Liberty Island, in recognition of the Statue's symbolic significance. The American Museum of Immigration, honoring those who chose these shores as their home, has been established in the base of the statue.

19
Thomas Jefferson Memorial

Washington, D.C.

"I have sworn upon the altar of God eternal hostility against every form of tyranny over the mind of man"

These words of Thomas Jefferson now indelibly inscribed in this memorial to him might be called the heart of his political and social thinking. His opposition to tyranny in all its forms was repeatedly voiced. In the Declaration of Independence it appears in his famous phrase "... that all men are created equal, that they are endowed by the Creator with certain inalienable rights..." It is seen in his Virginia Statute of Religious Freedom as "Well aware that Almighty God hath created the mind free;..." Elsewhere it is expressed in supporting his beliefs in a simple democratic form of government, freedom of the press, freedom of speech, and education of the masses. These principles and his leadership of the common man won for him the high place of third President of the United States. In this capacity he tried to insure these liberties by expanding the Nation's frontiers and political system to include the great Louisiana Territory. As an early champion of the natural and civic rights of the individual, which have remained the principal doctrines of Americanism, Thomas Jefferson will forever be remembered as one of the great figures in American history.

Jefferson, author of the Declaration of Independence, by that act alone would have been great; but he is included among the leviathans of American history because he gave a new emphasis and impetus to democracy in the United States. Foe of all kinds of human tyranny, as evidenced by his authorship of the Statute of Virginia for religious freedom and his opposition to the laws of primogeniture and entail, he fostered a democracy with a broader base and greater opportunity for higher education, mindful of the interests of the common man. He was an idealist, an architect and builder whose creative genius comprehended both physical structures and the molding of the political forms of the Republic. The most notable achievement of his two terms as President was the purchase of the vast Louisiana territory. The "Louisiana Purchase" more than doubled the land area of the young Nation. It opened new fields of economic opportunity for men of all classes and degrees of wealth, perpetuated for three-quarters of a century the constructive influences of the democratic frontier, and guaranteed the physical greatness and strength of the United States.

This memorial, built in a style of his own liking, is an appropriate tribute to Jefferson's contributions to the founding of the American Republic.

THE MEMORIAL SITE

A circular colonnaded structure of marble rises from the banks of the Tidal Basin as a memorial to the author of the Declaration of Independence. The classic beauty of the Thomas Jefferson Memorial is enhanced by its reflection in the waters of the Tidal Basin. The importance of Jefferson as one of the great figures in the Nation's history demanded a memorial site of prominence in the central plan of the Capital City and in relation to the other great memorials already built. The Capitol, the White House, and the Mall were located in accordance with the famous L'Enfant Plan. The lone remaining site in this cross-like scheme was the one selected for the Jefferson Memorial south of the Tidal Basin on a line with the south axis of the White House.

THE MEMORIAL BUILDING

The significance of the architectural scheme of the Thomas Jefferson Memorial is apparent to even the casual student of Jefferson. This building expresses the architectural preference of America's third President as shown in his famous home, Monticello, and is designed in the style of the circular-domed Pantheon of Rome, a structure Jefferson mentioned several times in his writings. In the preparation of the plan for the memorial the architects were clearly influenced by Jefferson's own taste. Thus, the circular colonnaded structure is an adaptation of the classic style which Jefferson himself is credited with having introduced into this country. It reflects even in its pattern a measure of the respect held by our Nation for this great American.

The entrance to the memorial is on the north, or Tidal Basin side. Over the entrance is a sculptural group depicting Jefferson before a committee appointed by the Continental Congress to draw up the Declaration of Independence.

On the interior walls of the memorial room are four panels carrying inscriptions based upon the writings of Jefferson describing the chief principles of his beliefs. On the southwest wall are famous and inspiring phrases from the Declaration of Independence. It is appropriate that these words should occupy the first panel in the sequence. It was Jefferson's wish that he be remembered first as the author of this most famed of American documents.

The words of the second panel embody his principle of freedom of the mind. It is nowhere better expressed than in his Virginia Statute for Religious Freedom upon which this panel is based.

The third panel is devoted to his ideas on freedom of the body and to his beliefs in the necessity of educating the masses of the people. Although his efforts to abolish slavery were not successful, he was one of the first Americans to argue forcefully the inconsistency of slavery in a democratic state. Jefferson considered his establishment of the University of Virginia as one of his outstanding accomplishments. Throughout his entire public career, he maintained that the general education of the people was necessary to efficient self-government.

Jefferson's vision in matters of government is demonstrated by the fourth panel. By this statement which appeared in a letter to a friend we know that he recognized the necessity for change in the laws and institutions of a democracy. This was especially true, he believed, as opinions altered, new discoveries were made, and circumstances changed.

The domed interior of the memorial is dominated by a heroic statue of Thomas Jefferson. Rudulph Evans, the sculptor, was chosen from more than a hundred who were considered in a nationwide competition conducted by the Thomas Jefferson Memorial Commission. The height of the statue is 19 feet, and it stands in the center of the memorial room upon a pedestal of black Minnesota granite reaching 6 feet above the floor. The statue of Jefferson, together with the inscriptions executed in bronze, is in pleasant contrast with the white Georgia marble of the interior. The 4 colonnaded openings of the memorial—2 on the east-west axis, and 2 on the north-south—make it possible to view the figure from many angles and with varying lights and shadows. The domed ceiling of Indiana limestone reaches approximately 67 feet above the head of the statue.

The exterior walls and dome of Danby Imperial Vermont marble reach approximately 96 feet above this level. The terraces and steps seen below are about 25 feet above the ground. The diameter of the building from this position is approximately 152 feet. From this walk, a visitor gets a glimpse of the Capitol, the White House, the Washington Monument, and the Lincoln Memorial.

CONSTRUCTION OF THE MEMORIAL

Provision for building an appropriate permanent memorial to Thomas Jefferson in the Capital City was made by act of Congress in 1934. John Russell Pope and the survivors of his firm, Otto R. Eggers and Daniel P. Higgins, designed the structure. Ground-breaking ceremonies were held on December 15, 1938, and the cornerstone was officially laid on November 15, 1939. On April 13, 1943, the memorial to Jefferson was dedicated.

ORIENTAL FLOWERING CHERRY TREES

In early spring, when the oriental flowering cherry trees are in bloom, the memorial appears in its most beautiful setting. The cherry trees were the gift of the city of Tokyo to the city of Washington. The blossoming of these famous trees, which encircle the Basin, depends upon seasonal conditions. They ordinarily bloom about the first week in April and remain so for 10 to 12 days. The annual Cherry Blossom Festival is staged near the memorial during this period. The pageantry of the Festival, the architectural splendor of the marble memorial, the inspirational beauty of the dainty pink blossoms, all combine to make a visit to the Jefferson Memorial a delightful and lasting memory.

Bronze statue of Thomas Jefferson
by sculptor Rudulph Evans is 19 feet high.

20
Tomb of the Unknown Soldier

Arlington, Va.

In beautiful Arlington National Cemetery in Virginia on a hillside overlooking the historic Potomac River is a shrine which has become a mecca for all Americans who visit Washington, and for many prominent dignitaries and persons from foreign lands as well. It is the Tomb of the Unknown Soldier, symbolizing those of America who gave their lives in World War I, World War II and in the Korean conflict.

Following the custom inaugurated by other allied countries in World War I, the Congress on March 4, 1921, approved a resolution providing for the burial in Arlington National Cemetery Memorial Amphitheater on Armistice Day 1921 of an unknown and unidentified American soldier of World War I. Against the background of the principal facade of the Memorial Amphitheater is the Tomb of the Unknown Soldier. Lying in a sarcophagus beneath the tomb is the body of an American hero of World War I. The story of how this soldier was selected is a poignant one.

In 1921, nearly three years after the end of World War I, six American soldiers, serving with the occupation forces in Germany, were recalled to France. They were directed to a chapel at Chalons-sur-Marne.

An American colonel met the young soldiers outside the chapel and said, "Men, it is my task to choose one of you to perform a great and sacred duty."

In his hand, the officer held a bouquet of roses. He turned to one of the six: Sergeant Edward Younger.

"In this church," he said, "are four caskets. In them lie the bodies of four nameless American soldiers. Go into the church. Put a rose on one of the caskets. That is all."

Younger told the rest of the story later:

"I went into the church and walked past the caskets. I walked around them three times. Suddenly I stopped. It was as though some-

80

thing had pulled me. A voice seemed to say: 'This is a pal of yours.'"

"I put the rose on the coffin in front of me and went back out into the sunlight. I still remember the awed feeling I had, standing there alone."

On May 30, 1958, the bodies of two Americans of World War II and the Korean conflict were returned to the United States and interred next to the Unknown Soldier.

The selection of a soldier from World War II was more complex due to the three combat areas involved—Europe, Africa and Asia. First on May 12, 1958, at Epinal American Cemetery in Epinal, France, an Unknown Soldier was chosen to represent the trans-Atlantic areas. Major General Edward J. O'Neill made the choice from thirteen candidates from Europe and Africa. Then on May 16, 1958, at Hickam Air Force Base, Honolulu, Hawaii, Colonel Glen T. Eagleston selected the soldier to represent the trans-Pacific areas. He chose from six soldiers, four who had fallen in the Philippines and two from Hawaii.

Finally on May 26, 1958, aboard the *Canberra,* Hospitalman First Class William R. Charette chose the Unknown Soldier of World War II. The caskets of the trans-Pacific and trans-Atlantic soldiers were placed on either side of the Korean Unknown— the latter having been chosen on May 15th by Master Sergeant Ned Lyle at the National Memorial Cemetery of the Pacific. Charette chose the casket to the right of the Korean soldier. Later that day both Unknown Soldiers were transferred to the *Blandy* and shipped to Washington, where on May 30th they were placed in Arlington Cemetery next to the Unknown Soldier of World War I.

In honoring these heroes of three wars, the Nation has paid tribute to the more than half million Americans who in three wars have died for their country—116,563 in World War I: 407,828 in World War II; and 54,246 in Korea.

The Tomb was designed by Lorimer Rich, and sculpted by Thomas Hudson Jones. The design of the Tomb is striking in its simplicity, being made of only four pieces of marble. The front panel is adorned with a composition of three symbolic figures commemorative of the spirit of the Allies. The rear panel bears the inscription: *Here rests in honored glory an American soldier known but to God.*

A guard of honor keeps a day and night vigil over the Tomb of the Unknowns. Members of the Tomb Guard are from or assigned to the Honor Guard Company of the 1st Battle Group 3rd Infantry (The Old Guard). They must meet rigid qualifications, present an outstanding soldierly appearance, and stand between 5' 10" and 6' 2" tall. They undergo special training for two or three months and if they measure up to the standards of the unit, they are awarded a distinctive badge of the Tomb Guard. When the cemetery is open to the public, on the hour there is a formal "changing of the guard." One cannot witness this brief and solemn ceremony without experiencing a surge of patriotic fervor, a poignant reminder of our indebtedness to those who gave all so that we might remain a free people.

Within the grounds of Arlington Cemetery, *by their Nation blessed,* sleep heroes of all our wars, from the days of the American Revolution to this day. So it will be as long as the Republic endures. Here in peace they rest, without regard to race, creed, faith, or color — a memorial symbol of the American way of life.

As a grateful Nation honors those who dedicated their lives to the glory of their country, so likewise we as individuals share the privilege of honoring those we loved who forever rest in this great sanctuary of valor and of devotion to country.

21 Washington Monument

Washington, D. C.

As a towering shaft, the Washington Monument has, since the late nineteenth century, dominated the Capital City's skyline. Its simplicity and innate dignity make it an appropriate memorial to our first President.

Washington was a big man. He stood 6 feet, 2 inches, broad of shoulder, long of limb, erect and muscular at 200 pounds. His strength was extraordinary and his walk was majestic. By common consent he was one of the best horsemen of the continent; when mounted for travel, for the hunt, or for the field of battle, he filled the eye.

And he was big in character. Thomas Jefferson described him as a man who was not an intellectual but whose judgment was sound and sure. "Perhaps the strongest feature of his character," Jefferson said, "was prudence, never acting until every circumstance, every consideration, was maturely weighed... His integrity was most pure, his justice the most inflexible I have ever known . . . He was indeed, in every sense of the words, a wise, a good and a great man... On the whole, his character was, in its mass, perfect, in nothing bad, in few points indifferent; and it may truly be said, that never did nature and fortune combine more perfectly to make a man great . . . ."

When he gave his confidence, he could be "talkative," as Jefferson, James Madison, and other friends attested. Although he did not possess a ready and spontaneous wit, Madison observed "he was particularly pleased with the jokes, good humor and hilarity of his companions."

The picture of George Washington as a cold, distant figure and a paragon of unmitigated virtue is a misconception that has tended to obscure his vigor, his wide-ranging interests, his kindness, and the warmth of his personality. As a soldier he was a rigid disciplinarian, not giving to "leveling" among ranks, but there is an account which relates that on mild days at Valley Forge he went out and pitched ball with his young aides, or, as one officer said, sometime "did us the honor to play wickets with us." Yes, he was a big man — and a big human being.

George Washington's life was not one of rags to riches, though it was to a large extent one of obscurity to renown. By the time he was born to Mary Ball and Augustine Washington, a well-to-do planter and ironmonger on Popes Creek in Virginia's Northern Neck, the Tidewater already supported a life of abundance and some elegance, patterned after the squirearchy of rural England.

George was 11 when his father died. For model and mentor he then took his urbane half-brother, Lawrence, 14 years his elder. He did not return "home" to England for an education as many of his contemporaries did, nor did he attend any of the colonial colleges. His formal education ended when he was 16. However, he learned to write an excellent hand, to spell reasonably well, to be proficient in mathematics, geography, and astronomy, and to know at least the rudiments of Latin and literature. And at 16, as an apprentice, he had learned the surveyor's trade.

Inordinately ambitious for wealth and eminence, George set out early in life to attain them. Like all Virginians of his class, he had an absorbing thirst for land; at 18 he acquired in the Shenandoah Valley his first acreage and eventually owned some 50,000 acres. At 21, as a path to distinction, he turned to "the military line." When he heard in 1753 that Gov. Robert Dinwiddie planned to send a courier to warn the French to stay out of English claims in the Ohio Valley, he volunteered for the mission. In November, he led a small party a thousand miles through the wintry wilderness to deliver the Governor's proclamation. He was fired on by an unfriendly "French" Indian and swept overboard from his raft into the angry, ice-clogged

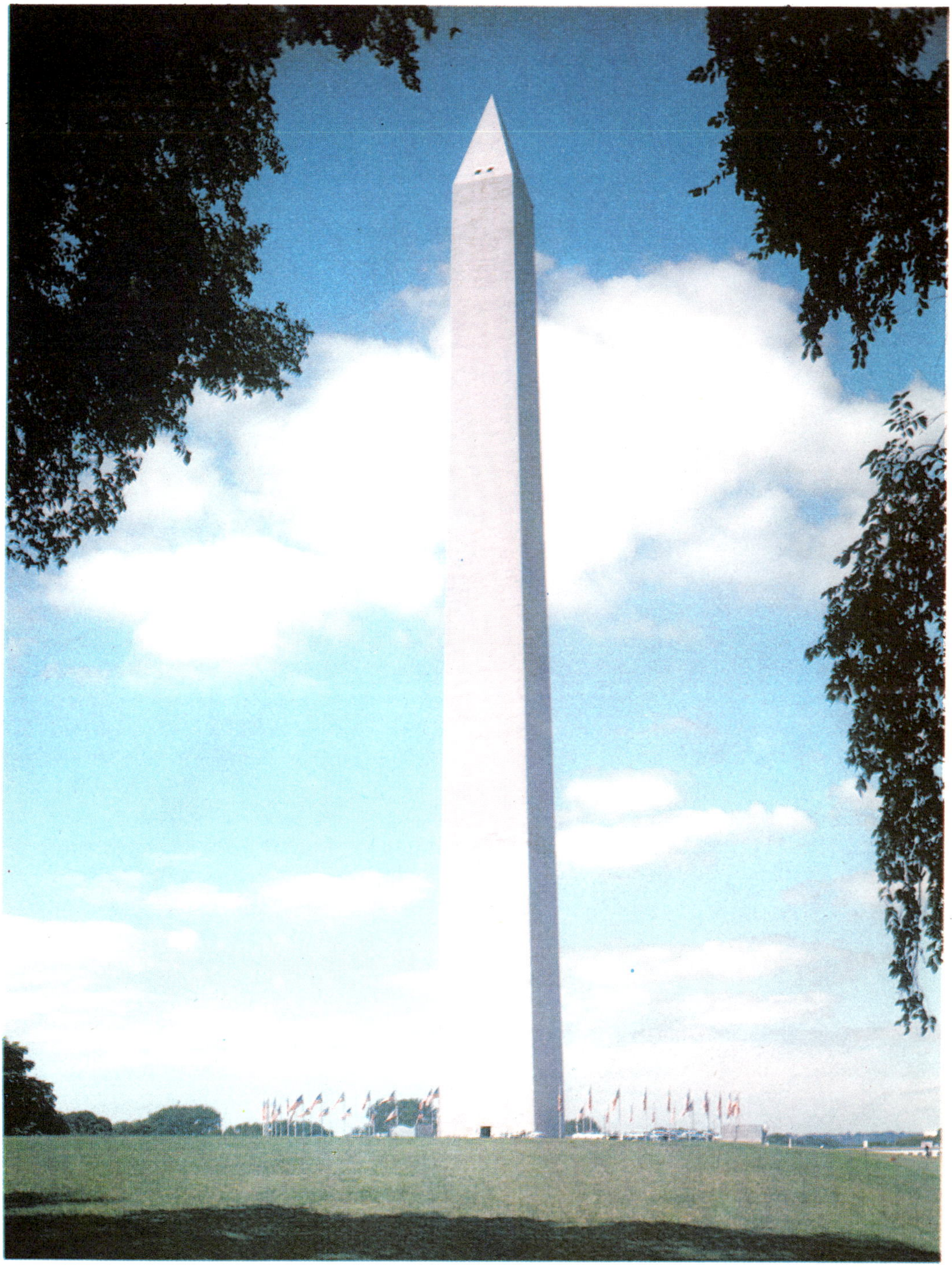

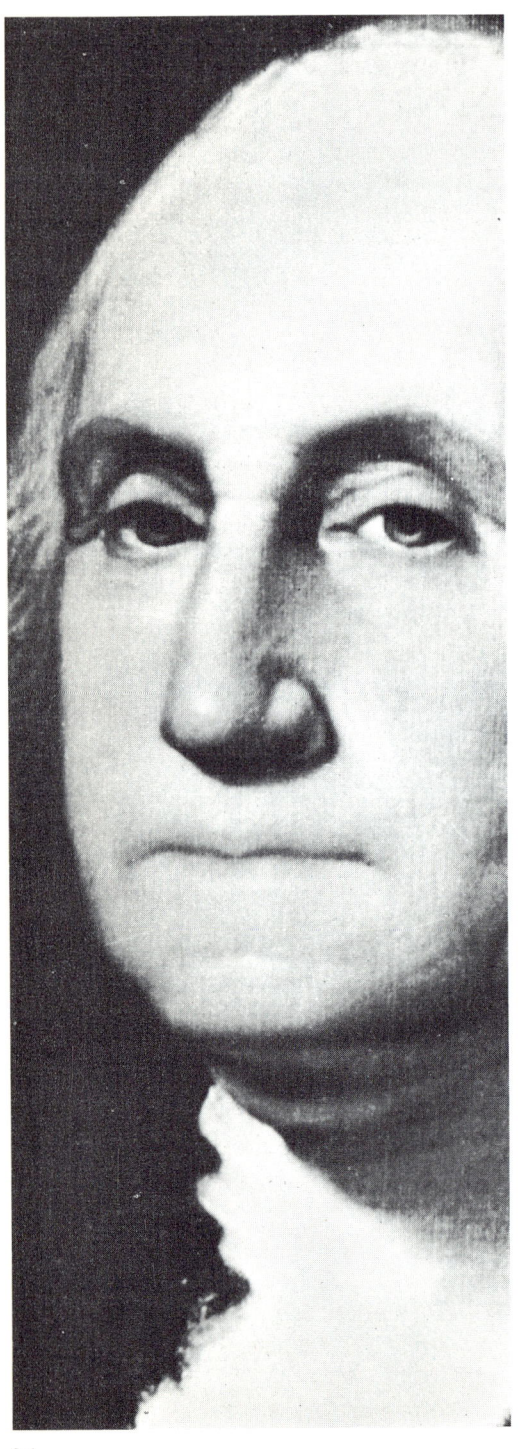

Allegheny River. But in January he was back in Williamsburg, having delivered Dinwiddie's message and taken an accurate measure of the French rivals at the forks of the Ohio. With the publication of his formal report in Williamsburg and London, his ascendency began.

The next year, elevated to a colonelcy, he led a military expedition against the French, who stubbornly refused to relinquish the Ohio country. And for the better part of the next 5 years he was engaged in warfare in the West. Although he distinguished himself in the disastrous Braddock expedition, the highly sensitive, ambitious young colonel, to whom bullets, he said, made a "charming" sound, was sufficiently discouraged by lack of recognition to resign his commission in December 1758, at age 26.

When in January 1759 he married lively, affable Martha Dandridge Custis, a 27-year-old widow with two children, he found the wife to whom he remained deeply devoted for over 40 years. For 15 years Washington lived happily at Mount Vernon, which he had inherited from Lawrence. He improved his plantation, increased his properties, and served as church vestryman, county justice, and member of the Virginia legislature. Like every colonial businessman during those years he chaffed under the ever harsher regulations of the British government. And when the first intercolonial Congress assembled in Philadelphia in September 1774 to consider united resistance to Britain, Washington was a delegate from Virginia.

The following spring he was sitting in the Second Continental Congress when word came from New England that a war had started there against the Crown. When the Congress resolved to "adopt" the New England army of farmers, shopkeepers, and mechanics, Colonel Washington was chosen unanimously as commander in chief. To the Congress he represented military experience (though his was limited), wisdom, and strength. For 8 years, making mistakes and profiting by them, holding together by the force of his will an often indifferent ragtag army, cajoling an often reluctant and discouraged Congress to support a seemingly hopeless war, Washington faithfully stood by his trust.

In time, his defensive war produced the stunning victory at Saratoga and brought France to the side of the embattled colonies. When Nathanael Greene, his personal choice for command in the South, drove Lord Charles Cornwallis' army into Virginia, Washington performed his most brilliant military feat. Cooperating with the French, he swiftly and secretly marched his army from the Hudson to Chesapeake Bay, took Cornwallis, and settled the issue of war.

At hostilities' end, after 8 years of absence from the place he loved, Washington looked forward to long, uninterrupted years on the banks of the Potomac. But within 4 years he again was called to his country's service. Washington, the Nation's most respected and adored hero, was a natural choice for President of the Constitutional Convention that met in 1787 to frame a government to replace the old, tottering Confederation. His presence, as always, gave stability to the convention deliberations, and encouraged the confidence of the Nation in the proceedings.

There was never any question in the minds of the people but that General Washington, who had first brought into being a new Nation, should become its first President. So again forsaking domestic tranquility, he assumed in 1789 the civil leadership of his country. With his remarkable sense of balance and perspective, he set about creating the office of President.

His accomplishments as President were enormous. He came to the office without a government; within a year he had a system set up and working. The departments had been organized, a revenue service established, Federal Courts formed, the postal service taken over, and a number of other functions of government set in motion. By the close of his administration he had established the relationships that continue to exist in large measure today between the branches of government. Declining a third term, Washington, now 64, returned to Mount Vernon, hoping once again to spend his declining years at home. There, on December 12, 1799, a raw, snowy day, he rode 5 hours about his farms and contracted an illness from which he was dead before 11 o'clock on the quiet winter night of the 14th.

George Washington's death cast the entire Nation into mourning. And when the news reached Europe, that continent, too, lamented. The London *Morning Chronicle* declared, "The long life of General Washington is not stained by a single blot . . . His fame, bounded by no country, will be confined to no age." Napoleon ordered a 10-day requiem throughout France. Dirges were played in Amsterdam. In America, President John Adams ordered the Army to wear crepe armbands for 6 months, and in cities and towns ladies donned black "as if for a relation." At Philadelphia, the Congress adjourned immediately and set December 26 as a day for formal mourning. That day from the pulpit of the Lutheran Church, Virginia Congressman Henry Lee, who had known Washington so well and so long, spoke publicly the words never forgotten, "First in war, first in peace, and first in the hearts of his countrymen."

HIS MONUMENT

A grieving and admiring Congress promptly resolved to erect a marble monument in the Capital City. The House passed a $200,000 appropriation, but the Senate considered the

85

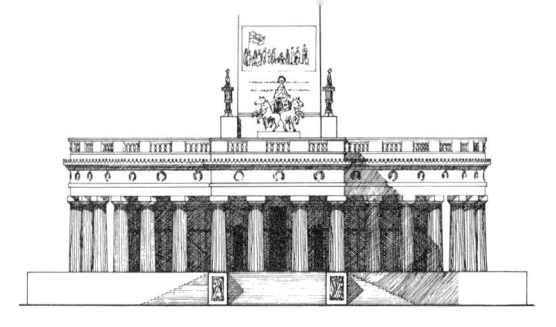

Robert Mills' original design for the Washington Monument called for a "grand circular colonnaded building" at the base.

measure a year, then let it die. For the next 33 years, except for an occasional fruitless expression of interest in the halls of Congress, the project languished.

Then in 1833, influential citizens of Washington city, led by George Watterston, who had been the first librarian of Congress, organized the Washington National Monument Society to raise by private subscription the memorial Congress had forgotten. From designs submitted in competition, that of Robert Mills, an eminent architect, was selected. It pictured a "grand circular colonnaded building" 259 feet in diameter and 100 feet high, from whose top rose a decorated Egyptian obelisk 500 feet high. Its total height of 600 feet would make it the highest spire in the world.

Dollar donations were solicited from the public, but response was disappointingly slow. It was not until 1847 that $87,000, a sum sufficient for a beginning, was raised. President James K. Polk, with the assent of Congress, selected the site on public lands, upwards of 30 acres, "so elevated that the Monument will be seen from all parts of the city," as indeed it is today. On the sunny Fourth of July 1848, Benjamin B. French, Grand Master of the District of Columbia Masonic Lodge, laid the cornerstone of the monument.

But as the monument began to rise, funds dwindled. Along with appeals for further funds, the Society invited each of the States to furnish for mounting in the interior walls a block of native stone, and later extended the invitation to municipalities, organizations, and foreign powers. Inscribed stones were enthusiastically shipped into Washington—and one brought about a long halt and almost an end to the erection of the monument.

From the Temple of Concord in Rome, Pope Pius IX sent a stone. About 1 o'clock in the morning of March 7, 1854, several members of the anti-immigrant, anti-Catholic Know-Nothing Party, which had sprung into being in the 40's, tied the night watchman at the monument in his watch box, stole the Pope's gift from its shed, and presumably smashed it and flung it into the Potomac. An outraged Nation curtailed its donations, funds ran out, and the huffing of the steam hoist and the creaking of the derrick at the monument were stilled. The Monument Society appealed desperately to the Congress for financial aid, and Congress agreed to appropriate $200,000. But the next spring, while the grant was being considered, the Know Nothings illegally elected a new slate of officers of the society and seized possession of the monument and its records. Congress tabled its resolution. For nearly 4 years, until it collapsed as a political entity, the Know-Nothing Party kept possession of the unfinished monument. Hoping to raise $1,000,000, it received from its members only $51.66, and could do no more than put on two courses of inferior stone which later had to be removed.

The rude incursion of the Know-Nothings, for all its threat to the monument, was as nothing compared to the sundering of the Nation in those years of the 1850's. The approaching catastrophe of civil war was subtly reflected in the inscriptions on the tribute stones. The Delaware inscription read, "First to Adopt, Will be the last to Desert the Constitution." Michigan sent her block of copper engraved as "An Emblem of Her Trust in the Union." Louisiana, an early contributor, proclaimed herself, "Ever Faithful to the Constitution and the Union." But other Southern States, as the divisive years moved toward their fiery culmination at Fort Sumter, were more equivocal. Georgia's stone arrived bearing the motto, "The Union as it was, The Constitution as it is." While Missouri offered her stone "To the Memory of Washington and a Pledge of her Fidelity to the Union of the States," Mississippi simply saluted "The Father of His Country." Proud, embittered South Carolina and several others carved on their stones only their State seals. These stones dot the landings today, serving as memorials not only to Washington but also to union, disunion, and reunion.

When civil war overtook the country in 1861, the 150-foot stub of the monument stood dejected amidst construction debris and the evil-smelling marshes stretching out from its base. After the war, there were national wounds to heal, and the monument remained forsaken, a sorry spectacle, surmounted by its silent derrick weathering in the sun, wind and rain.

By the time 1876 arrived and the Nation celebrated the centennial of American Independence, Congress was once again inspired to action and appropriated $200,000 for completion of the monument. Over the years, Robert Mills' original design had been modified piecemeal; now it was discarded entirely for a simple, traditionally proportioned but impressive obelisk 555 feet 5⅛ inches high.

When Army engineers took over in 1880, they discovered that the structure had tilted very slightly. Carefully it was shored up and a new slab of concrete, 13½ feet thick, laid under the old foundations. The faces of the 150-foot unfinished shaft were found not to aline with the points of the compass, so a slight "twist" was given the construction to bring the upper surfaces into the planes of the compass. The Corps of Engineers, during its first working season, was unable for a time to obtain Maryland marble like that used to face the first 150 feet, so 26 feet of Massachusetts marble were laid. At the 176-foot level, the Engineers were able again to obtain Maryland marble. The courses of Massachusetts marble weathered to a slightly different tone, which accounts for the "ring" noticeable on the shaft.

At last on December 6, 1884, in a howling gale, the capstone was set, the aluminum tip placed, and it was finished — an 81,120-ton hollow shaft which had taken 36 years, 5 months, and 2 days to build. Since Washington's birthday, an appropriate date, fell on Sunday in 1885, the monument was dedicated on Saturday, February 21. President Chester A. Arthur accepted it "in behalf of the people." Three years later, the Washington Monument was opened to the public.

The tall white marble obelisk is 55 feet 1½ inches wide at its base, and 34 feet 5½ inches wide at the top of the shaft. Its hollow column is topped by a marble pyramid, an aluminum cap, and 144 platinum-tipped lightning conductors. The immense structure weighs 90,854 tons. Eight hundred and ninety-eight steps lead to a chamber within the base of the pyramidal top. Along this stairway are the memorial stones. Mixed with the State stones are those from organizations and municipalities. On the first landing the Franklin Fire Company of Washington, D. C., advertises, "We Strive to Save." On the 17th landing all the stones are from foreign nations. On the 25th landing a stone from the employees of R. Norris & Son Locomotive Works of Philadelphia incongruously shares honors with a stone from the Alexandrian Library of ancient Egypt. As late as 1935, Hawaii added a stone. In using the stairway, one can view 190 tribute blocks set in the inner walls of the shaft.

From the beginning there has been a passenger elevator in the shaft, first a steam lift and today an electric car which whisks visitors to the top in 70 seconds. From the eight barred windows at the summit, the visitor has a majestic view of the District of Columbia and parts of Maryland and Virginia. Below him spreads the Federal City of Washington's dreams, a gem of capitals for a Nation shaped and guided by his hand.

22
Wright Brothers Memorial

Kitty Hawk, N.C.

The two persons who were to be the first to fly were born in the Midwest shortly after the Civil War: Wilbur Wright on April 16, 1867, near New Castle, Ind.; Orville Wright on August 19, 1871, in Dayton, Ohio. They were the sons of Milton Wright, a minister of the United Brethren Church. As boys they shared a common interest in mechanical devices. When they first began to think of trying to fly, they were operating the Wright Cycle Co., in Dayton, manufacturing, selling, and repairing bicycles.

Always interested in science, they were much impressed by the gliding experiments in Germany of Otto Lilienthal, the father of gliding and the first to explain scientifically why curved surfaces in a flying machine are superior to flat surfaces. The Wrights always considered Lilienthal their greatest inspiration. They believed that a glider should be built in a way that the right and left wings could be presented at different angles to the wind for sidewise balance, and they determined to do this by warping or twisting the wings. To try their scheme for control, they built a 5-foot model of a glider and, one day in 1899, tested it. Then they started thinking of a place for testing a man-carrying glider. After a study of wind records obtained from the Weather Bureau at Washington, they picked Kitty Hawk. During their first stay there in September 1900, they camped in a tent. Returning the next year with a larger glider, they built a camp a few hundred feet north of Kill Devil Hill. In their gliding experiments of 1900 and 1901 they got less lifting power from the wings than existing tables of air pressures on curved surfaces had led them to expect. This caused them to believe that all of these tables must be wrong.

After their return to Dayton, experiments led them to new knowledge about wing design. In a small wind tunnel, they tested more than 200 types of miniature wing surfaces.

Among other things, these experiments proved the fallacy of a sharp leading edge of an airplane wing and the inefficiency of deeply cambered wings, then generally advocated. In a few weeks they accomplished work of almost incalculable importance. Not only were they the first to test miniature wings accurately, they were the first in the world to compile tables of figures from which one might design an airplane that could fly. The Wright brothers' wind-tunnel experiments marked a turning point in the efforts of man to conquer the air. The brothers returned to Kill Devil Hills in 1902 with a glider having a wingspan of 32 feet, built according to their own figures on wind pressure. It was soon evident that this 1902 glider showed a great advance over any other ever built. In it, they made many glides of more than 600 feet against a 36-mile-an-hour wind. No previous experimenter had ever dared try to glide in so stiff a wind.

The next year they built both *The Flyer*, a craft with a wingspan of more than 40 feet, and the powerplant, a 12-horsepower engine, weighing 200 pounds. Its two propellers, designed according to their own calculations, were the first predictable performance propellers ever built. Machine and pilot together weighed about 750 pounds.

THE FIRST FLIGHT

It was late in September 1903 when the Wrights reached their camp at Kill Devil Hills. Delayed by mechanical problems and bad weather, they were not ready until December 14 to fly their machine. The first trial was not quite successful. Without enough wind to start from level ground, they took the machine to the slope of the hill where they placed the sledlike skids on a "truck"—a plank about 6 feet long, with rollers—which rested on a monorail track. Wilbur won the toss of a coin for what he called the "first whack." When *The Flyer* left the track and before it had gained enough speed, Wilbur turned it upward too suddenly. It climbed a few feet, stalled, and settled to the ground near the foot of the hill after being in the air just 3½ seconds. One of the skids and several other parts were broken. Two days were needed for making repairs.

On the morning of December 17, the wind blew at 22 to 27 miles an hour. Hoping it would die down, the Wrights waited. When it continued, they decided to go ahead and attempt a flight. On a smooth stretch of level ground just west of their camp, they laid a 60-foot track, pointing directly into the wind. (The takeoff spot is now marked by a granite boulder.) By the time all was ready, three men from the Kill Devil Hills Lifesaving Station and two others had arrived. It was now Orville's turn. Before climbing aboard the machine, he put his camera on a tripod and asked John T. Daniels of the U.S. Lifesaving Crew to press the button when the machine had risen directly in front of the camera. Nestled in the control mechanism on the lower wing, Orville started the machine down the track, traveling slowly into a 27-mile-an-hour headwind. After running 40 feet on the track, the plane took off, climbed about 10 feet in the air, darted erratically up and down several times, and dipped suddenly to earth about 120 feet from takeoff point.

As Orville Wright put it: "This flight lasted only 12 seconds, but it was nevertheless the first in history in which a machine carrying a man had raised itself by its own power into the air in full flight, had sailed forward without reduction of speed, and finally landed at a point as high as that from which it started." The brothers alternated in making three more flights that morning, each longer than the previous one; on the fourth flight, Wilbur flew 852 feet in 59 seconds. As it seemed imprudent to fly at much height at

The first flight — December 17, 1903, with Orville Wright at the controls.

first, it was sometimes impossible to correct the up and down motion of the machine before it struck the ground. This accounts for the flights being so short. While the Wrights and onlookers were discussing the flights, a gust of wind struck the plane and rolled it over, damaging it badly. It could not be repaired in time for any more flights that year; in fact it never flew again.

AFTER THE FIRST FLIGHT

After 1903, the Wrights carved brilliant careers in aeronautics and helped found the aviation industry. The successful flights made at Kill Devil Hills in December 1903 encouraged them to make improvements on a new plane called Flyer No. 2. About 100 flights were flown near Dayton in 1904.

A new and improved plane, Flyer No. 3, was built in 1905. On October 5 they made a record flight of 24 1/5 miles, while the plane was in the air 38 minutes and 3 seconds. The era of the airplane was well on the way. The lessons and successes at Kill Devil Hills in December 1903 were fast making the crowded skies of the Air Age possible.

Believing their invention was now perfected for practical use, the Wrights wanted the United States Government to have a world monopoly on their patents, and more important, on all the aerodynamic, design, and pilotage secrets they knew relating to the airplane. As early as 1905 they had received overtures from representatives of foreign governments. The United States Army turned down their first offers without making an effort to investigate whether the airplane had been brought to a stage of practical operation. But disbelief was on the wane. In February 1908 the United States War Department made a contract with the brothers for an airplane. Only 3 weeks later the Wrights closed a contract with a Frenchman to form a syndicate for the rights to manufacture, sell, or license the use of the Wright airplane in France.

During their Dayton experiments, the Wrights had continued to pilot their airplanes while lying prone with hips in the cradle on the lower wing. Now they adopted a different arrangement of the control levers to be used in a sitting position and added a seat for a passenger. The brothers brought their airplane to Kill Devil Hills in April 1908 to practice handling the new arrangement of the control levers. They wanted to be prepared for the public trials to be made for the United States Government, near Washington, and for the company in France.

They erected a new building at Kill Devil Hills to house the airplane and to live in, because storms the year before had nearly demolished their 1903 camp buildings. Between May 6 and May 14, 1908, the Wrights made 22 flights at their old testing grounds. On May 14 the first flight with two men aboard a plane was made near West Hill; Wilbur Wright being the pilot, and Charles Furnas, a mechanic, the passenger. Orville and Furnas then made a flight together of over 2 miles passing between Kill Devil Hill and West Hill, and turning north near the sound to circle Little Hill before returning over the starting point to land near West Hill on the second lap.

Byron R. Newton, a newspaper reporter, was concealed in the woods with other newsmen near camp to watch the Wrights fly. Newton predicted in his diary just after seeing his first flight: "Some day Congress will erect a monument here to these Wrights." Nineteen years later the Congress established the area as a National Memorial.

THE NATIONAL MEMORIAL

On March 2, 1927, the Congress authorized the establishment of Kill Devil Hills Monument National Memorial to commemorate the Wrights' achievement of the first successful flight of a man-carrying, power-driven, heavier-than-air machine. The area was transferred from the War Department to the National Park Service, U.S. Department of the Interior, on August 10, 1933, and on December 1, 1953, the name was changed to Wright Brothers National Memorial. The Memorial contains about 425 acres. It embraces the actual site of the first four flights and the sites of most of the glider experiments.

Two wooden structures built by the National Park Service in 1953 on the 50th anniversary of the first flight are reconstructions of the Wright brothers' 1903 living quarters and hangar based on historical research and photographs of the originals. The furnishings within the living quarters are of the 1902-3 period, and are almost exact duplications of those used by the Wrights.

A 10-ton granite memorial boulder was placed by the National Aeronautic Association in 1928 on the 25th anniversary of the first flight. The boulder marks the take-off point of the first flight and of the three additional flights made December 17, 1903.

Atop Kill Devil Hill stands the striking Wright memorial shaft, a triangular pylon 60 feet high, made of gray granite from Mount Airy, N. C. Construction was begun February 4, 1931, and the shaft was dedicated November 19, 1932. Its sides ornamented with outspread wings in bas-relief, the pylon gives to the eye the impression of a gigantic bird about to take off into space. West Hill, the sand dune which was the scene of many of the Wrights' gliding experiments in 1901-03, was stabilized with grasses adapted to sandy soil by the National Park Service in 1934 to preserve the historic site.

Index

Adams, John, 41, 85
Adams, Samuel, 60-61
Albany (N.Y.), 66-68
Allentown (Pa.), 44
American Museum of
  Immigration (N.Y.), 75
American Revolution, 19-20, 30, 32,
  40-42, 44, 60-63, 66-69
Anderson, Maj. Robert, 26-29
Appomattox Court House (Va.),
  10-11
Argall, Sir Samuel, 49
Arlington National Cemetery
  (Va.), 80-81
Armistead, Maj. George, 24
Armistead, Gen. Lewis, 36
Arnold, Gen. Benedict, 68-69
Arthur, Chester A., 87
Articles of Confederation, 42
Ashley, William H., 50
Assembly, Provincial (Pa.), 40-44
Association for the Preservation
  of Virginia Antiquities, 48
Babcock, Lt. Col. Orville E., 11
Bacon, Henry, 52
Bacon, Nathaniel, 47
Bairstow, Ernest C., 53
Balcarres Redoubt (Saratoga), 69
Ball, Mary, 31-32, 82
Baltimore (Md.), 20-25
Barber Farm (Saratoga), 68
Barney, Comm. Joshua, 22
Barrett, Col. James, 61-62
Bartholdi, Frederick Auguste,
  71-72, 74
Basketmaker Indians, 56-58
Beanes, Dr., 25
Beauregard, Gen. P.G.T., 27-29
Bedloe's Island (N.Y.), 73-74
Bemis Heights (N.Y.), 67-68
Bennett, Richard, 49
Bennington, Battle of (Vt.), 67
Benton, Sen. Thomas Hart, 51
Berkeley, Sir William, 47-49
Bill of Rights, 18-19
Black Hills (S. Dak.), 64
Bladensburg (Md.), 22
Blodgett's Hotel (D.C.), 13
Borglum, Gutzon, 64-65
Borglum, Lincoln, 65
Boston (Mass.), 40, 60, 62-63
Braddock expedition, 84
Breymann Redoubt (Saratoga), 69
Brick Capitol (D.C.), 13, 17
Bridges Creek plantation
  (Va.), 30-32
Brooke, Col. Arthur, 23-24
Brumidi, Constantino, 14-15
Buchanan, James, 26'
Bulfinch, Charles, 13
Burgesses, House of, 47, 49
Burgoyne, Gen. John, 66-69
Butler, Jane, 31
Cambridge (Mass.), 63
Capitol Building (Washington),
  12-17, 77-78
Carpenters' Hall (Philadelphia), 41
Carson, Kit, 64
Cashtown (Pa.), 34
Cemetery Hill and Ridge
  (Gettysburg), 34-36
Central Pacific Railroad, 38-39
Chalons-sur-Marne (France), 80
Champlain, Lake, 66
Charette, William R., 81

Charleston (S.C.), 26-29
Charlestown (Mass.), 61, 63
Charter of Privileges, 44
Cherry Blossom Festival, 78
Chicago and Northwestern
  Railroad, 38
Chouteau, René and Jean, 50
City Hall (N.Y.), 18-19
Civil War, 10-11, 26-29, 32,
  34-36, 38, 44
Cleveland, Grover, 74
Cliff dwellings (Mesa Verde), 59
Cliff Palace (Mesa Verde), 58-59
Clinton, Sir Henry, 66, 68
Cochrane, Vice Adm. Alexander,
  22, 24-25
Cockburn, Rear Adm. George, 13, 22
Colonial Dames of America, 48
Committee of Vigilance
  and Safety, 22
Concord (Mass.), 41, 60-63
Congress, First, 18-19, 41, 84-85
Congress, Houses of, 14
Constitution, U.S., 18-19, 42
Constitutional Convention,
  18-19, 21, 42, 85
Continental Congress, First, 19, 41, 77
Continental Congress, Second,
  18-19, 41, 84
Coolidge, Calvin, 64
Cornwallis, Lord Charles, 85
Credit Mobilier investigation, 38
Culp's Hill (Gettysburg), 35-36
Cummings Point (S.C.), 26-28
Custis, George Washington Parke, 32
Custis, Martha Dandridge, 84
Custom House (N.Y.), 19
Dahlgren, Adm. John A. B., 29
Dale, Sir Thomas, 47
Daniels, John T., 89
Dawes, William, 61
Dayton (Ohio), 88, 90
Declaration of Independence,
  15, 19, 41-43, 76-77
Diamond, William, 61
Dinwiddie, Gov. Robert, 82
Discovery, 47
Doubleday, Capt. Abner, 27
Durant, Dr. Thomas, 39
Dutch Stadt Huys (N.Y.), 18
Eads Bridge (St. Louis), 51
Eagleston, Col. Glen T., 81
Eggers, Otto R., 78
Eiffel, Gustave, 72
Elizabethtown (Ky.), 8
Evans, Rudulph, 78
Everett, Edward, 44
Ewell, Gen. Richard, 35
Far View House (Mesa Verde), 58
Federal Hall (N.Y.), 18-19
Federal Reserve Bank (N.Y.), 19
Five Forks (Va.), 10
The Flyers, 89-90
Fort Babcock (Md.), 24
Fort Covington (Md.), 24
Fort Johnson (S.C.), 26-27
Fort McHenry (Md.), 20-25
Fort Moultrie (S.C.), 26-28
Fort Stanwix (N.Y.), 66
Fort Sumter (S.C.), 26-29
Fort Ticonderoga (N.Y.), 66
Fort Whetstone (Md.), 21
Fort Wood (N.Y.), 73
Fountain Inn (Baltimore), 25
Franco-American Union, 71, 74

Franklin, Benjamin, 41
Fraser, Gen. Simon, 69
Freeman Farm, 67-69
French, Benjamin B., 86
French, Daniel Chester, 52-55, 63
French traders, 50-51
Furnas, Charles, 90
Gage, Gen. Thomas, 60, 63
Gates, Gen. Horatio, 67-69
Gateway Arch (St. Louis), 51
Germain, George, 66
Gettysburg Address (Lincoln), 34, 53
Gettysburg Battlefield (Pa.), 34-36
Gillmore, Brig. Gen. Quincy, 29
Godspeed, 47
Golden Spike Historic Site
  (Utah), 38-39
Gordon, Gen. John B., 11
Grant, Gen. Ulysses S., 10-11
Great Redoubt (Saratoga), 69
Greene, Nathanael, 85
Guerin, Jules, 52
Hamilton, Andrew, 18, 40
Hancock, John, 61
Hancock, Gen. Winfield Scott, 34, 36
Hanks, Nancy, 8-9
Harding, Warren G., 52
Harrisburg (Pa.), 42
Hartwell, Henry, 49
Harvey, John, 49
Henry, Cape, 46, 49
Hickam A.F.B. (Honolulu), 81
Higgins, Daniel P., 78
Hodgen's Mill (Ky.), 8
Hood, Gen. John B., 29, 35
Hooker, Gen. Joseph, 34
Hough, Pvt. Daniel, 28
House of Representatives, 13-14,
  16-17
Howe, Sir William, 66
Hudson River (N.Y.), 66-68
Hunt, Rev. Robert, 49
Hunter, Maj. Gen. D. H., 28
Independence (Mo.), 51
Independence Hall (Philadelphia),
  40-45
Jackson, Andrew, 17
James River (Va.), 47-48
Jamestown (Va.), 46-49
Jaquelin-Ambler House
  (Jamestown), 49
Jefferson, Thomas, 13, 41, 50-51,
  64, 76-78, 82
Jefferson Memorial (D.C.), 76-78
Jefferson National Expansion
  Memorial (Mo.), 50-51
Jenkins Hill (D.C.), 12-13
Johnston, Gen. Joseph E., 10
Jones, David, 31
Jones, Richard Lloyd, 9
Jones, Thomas Hudson, 81
Jupiter (engine), 39
Kemp, Richard, 49
Key, Francis Scott, 20, 24-25
Kill Devil Hills (N.C.), 88-91
Kitty Hawk (N.C.), 88
Knob Creek Farm (Ky.), 8
Know-Nothing Party, 86
Kosciuszko, Thaddeus, 67
Korean Unknown Soldier, 81
Korean War, 80-81
Laboulaye, Edouard de, 71
Lafayette, Marquis de, 44-45
Lancaster (Pa.), 42
Lazarus, Emma, 71

92

Learned, Gen. Ebenezer, 68-69
Lee, Gen. Fitzhugh, 11
Lee, Henry, 85
Lee, Richard Henry, 41
Lee, Gen. Robert E., 10-11, 34-36
Lee, Gov. Thomas S., 21
L'Enfant, Major Pierre Charles, 12-13, 19, 77
Lesseps, Count Ferdinand de, 74
Lester, Thomas, 44
Lexington (Mass.), 41, 61-63
Liberty Bell, 40, 44-45
Liberty Island (N.Y.), 73, 75
Lilienthal, Otto, 88
Lincoln, Abraham, 8-9, 14, 16, 26, 28, 34, 38, 52-55, 64
Lincoln, Sarah, 8
Lincoln, Thomas, 8-9
Lincoln (Mass.), 61, 63
Lincoln Birthplace, 8-9
Lincoln Memorial, 52-55, 78
Lisa, Manuel, 50
Little Pigeon Creek (Ind.), 9
Livingston, Robert R., 41
Long House (Mesa Verde), 58
Longman, Evelyn Beatrice, 53
Longstreet, Gen. James, 35-36
Louisiana Purchase, 50-51, 76-77
Ludwell, Philip, 48
Lukens, Isaiah, 44
Lyle, Sgt. Ned, 81
Madison, James, 13, 21, 42, 82
Marshall, Col. Charles, 11
Marshall, John, 45
Mattox Creek (Va.), 31
McHenry, James, 20-21
McLean House (Appomattox), 11
Meade, Gen. George G., 34-36
Memorial Amphitheater (Arlington), 80
Menotomy (Arlington) (Mass.), 63
Meriam's Corner (Mass.), 62-63
Mesa Verde (Colo.), 56-59
Mills, Robert, 43, 86-87
Minute Man Statue (Concord), 60-63
Monroe, James, 17
Monticello (Va.), 77
Morgan, Col. Daniel, 67-68
Morris Island (S.C.), 28-29
Mount Rushmore, Mount (S. Dak.), 64-65
Mount Vernon (Va.), 16, 31, 84-85
Napier, Capt., 24
Napoleon, 50, 85
National Memorial Cemetery of the Pacific, 81
New York (N.Y.), 18-19, 40, 42, 66, 68, 71-75
New York "World", 73
North Bridge (Concord), 61-63
Northern Virginia, Army of, 34, 36
North Point (Md.), 23
Northwest Ordinance, 18-19
Ogden (Utah), 39
Omaha (Nebr.), 38
119 (engine), 39
O'Neill, Maj. Gen. Edward J., 81
Ord, Gen. E.O.C., 11
Oriskany, Battle of (N.Y.), 66
Parker, John, 61
Patapsco River (Md.), 20, 22-23, 25
Patuxent River (Md.), 22
Peach Orchard (Gettysburg), 35-36
Peale, Charles Willson, 43
Peale, Rembrandt, 16
Penn, William, 44
Percy, Hugh (Earl), 63

Philadelphia (Pa.), 18-19, 40-45, 66, 85
Philosophical Hall (Philadelphia), 43
Piccirilli Brothers, 54-55
Pickett, Gen. George, 36
Pitcairn, Maj. John, 61, 63
Pit houses (Mesa Verde), 58-59
Pocahontas, 47, 49
Polk, James K., 86
Poor, Gen. Enoch, 68
Pope, Anne, 31
Pope, John Russell, 9, 52, 78
Pope, Col. Nathaniel, 31
Pope Pius IX, 86
Popes Creek plantation (Va.), 30-32, 82
Potomac, Army of the, 10, 34, 36
Potomac Park (D.C.), 52
Powhatan, 47
Prayer Room (Capitol Bldg.), 16
Prescott, Dr. Samuel, 61
Princeton (N.J.), 42
Promontory Summit (Utah), 38-39
Pueblo Indians, 57-59
Pulitzer, Joseph, 73
Punkatasset Hill (Concord), 61
Raleigh, Sir Walter, 46
Revere, Paul, 61
Revolutionary War, 19-20, 30, 32, 40-42, 44, 60-63, 66-69
Reynolds, Gen. John F., 34
Rich, Lorimer, 81
Rivardi, John Jacob Ulrich, 21
Robinson, Doane, 64
Rockefeller, John D., Jr., 33
Rodgers, Comm. John., 23
Rodman, Dr. George, 9
Rolfe, John, 47
Rolfe, Thomas, 47
Roosevelt, Franklin D., 17
Roosevelt, Theodore, 64
Ross, Maj. Gen. Robert, 22-23, 25
Round Tops (Gettysburg), 35
Rushmore, Mount (S. Dak.), 64-65
Saarinen, Eero, 51
Sacramento (Calif.), 38
St. Leger, Col. Barry, 66
St. Louis (Mo.), 50-51
Saratoga Battlefield (N.Y.), 66-69, 85
Sayler's Creek (Va.), 10
Schuyler, Gen. Philip, 66-67, 69
Schuylerville (N.Y.), 67, 69
Scott, Dred, 51
Secessionville (S.C.), 28
Seminary Ridge (Gettysburg), 36
Senate, 13-17
Sherman, Roger, 41
Sherman, Gen. William T., 29
Sickles, Gen. Daniel, 35
Sierra Nevada, 39
Sinking Spring Farm (Ky.), 8-9
Skinner, Col. John, 25
Smith, Lt. Col. Francis, 61-63
Smith, Capt. John, 47, 49
Smith, Maj. Gen. Samuel, 22-23
Spangler's Spring (Gettysburg), 35-36
Spruce Tree House (Mesa Verde), 58
Square Tower Touse (Mesa Verde), 58
Stamp Act Congress, 18-19
Stanford, Leland, 39
Star of the West, 26
Stark, Gen. John, 67
Star-Spangled Banner, 24-25

State House (Philadelphia), 40-45
Statuary Hall (Capitol Bldg.), 14
Statue of Freedom (Capitol Bldg.), 13-14
Statue of Liberty (N.Y.), 71-75
Stillwater (N.Y.), 67
Stone, Gen. Charles P., 73-74
Stricker, Brig. Gen. John, 23
Strickland, William, 44
Stuart, Gen. J.E.B., 34, 36
Sublette, William L., 50
Sub-Treasury (N.Y.), 19
Sumter, Thomas, 26
Supreme Court, 13-14, 17-19
Susan Constant, 47
Syng, Philip, 40
Taft, William Howard, 52
Thomas Jefferson Memorial (D.C.), 76-78
Thornton, Dr. William, 13
Tidal Basin (D.C.), 77-78
Tomb of the Unknown Soldier, 80-81
Tousard, Maj. Louis, 21
Transcontinental railroad, 38-39
Truman, Harry, 17
Trumbull, John, 15
Union Pacific Railroad, 38-39
University of Virginia, 78
Unknown Soldier, 80-81
Valley Forge (Pa.), 82
Virginia Company, 46-47
Virginia Statute of Religious Freedom, 76, 78
Wakefield plantation (Va.), 31-33
War of 1812, 20-26
Warner, Mildred, 31
Warner, Col. Seth, 67
Washington, Augustine, 30-33, 82
Washington, Augustine, Jr., 31-32
Washington, Butler, 31
Washington, George, 12-13, 16, 18-19, 21, 30-33, 42, 45, 64, 82, 84-87
Washington, Jane, 31
Washington, John, 30-31
Washington, John A., 16
Washington, Lawrence, 31, 82, 84
Washington, Lewis W., 32
Washington, Martha, 16, 32, 84
Washington, Mary Ball, 30
Washington, William Augustine, 32
Washington (D.C.), 12-17, 19, 22, 24-25, 42, 52-55, 76-78, 82, 84-87
Washington Monument, 78, 82, 84-87
Washington's Birthplace (Va.), 30-33
West Hill (N.C.), 90
Westmoreland County (Va.), 30-31
Westport (Mo.), 51
Whetstone Point (Md.), 20
White House, 12, 17, 77-78
Wigfall, Col. Louis T., 28
Wilbank, John, 44
Wilderness Road, 50
Wimar, Carl, 51
Woolley, Edmund, 40
World War I, 80-81
World War II, 80-81
Wright Brothers (Orville and Wilbur), 88-91
Wyatt, Sir Francis, 49
Yeardley, Sir George, 49
Yonge, Col. Samuel H., 49
Younger, Sgt. Edward, 80
Zenger, John Peter, 18
Zion Reformed Church (Allentown), 44

▲ MOUNT RUSHMORE

▲ GOLDEN SPIKE
HISTORIC SITE

MESA VERDE
▲ CLIFF DWELLINGS

© Copyright HAMMOND INCORPORATED, Maplewood, N. J.